The Great Northern Railway

An Irish Railway Pictorial

Tom Ferris

Midland Publishing

The Great Northern Railway, An Irish Railway Pictorial
Tom Ferris © 2003

ISBN 1 85780 169 5

First published in 2003 by Midland Publishing
4 Watling Drive, Hinckley, Leics, LE10 3EY, England.
Tel: 01455 233747   Fax: 01455 233737
E-mail: midlandbooks@compuserve.com

Design concept and layout, © Midland Publishing and
Stephen Thompson Associates

Midland Publishing is an imprint of
Ian Allan Publishing Ltd.

Printed in England by Ian Allan Printing Ltd
Molesey Road, Hersham, Surrey, KT12 4RG

Front cover: **For many, the 'Enterprise Express' which ran non-stop between Belfast and Dublin represented the GNR at its very best. On 20th May 1949 the train approaches Adavoyle summit hauled by VS class 4-4-0 No 208 *Lagan*.**
John Dewing.

Title page: **On Sunday 29th June 1956, a special train, bringing supporters to a big Gaelic football match at Clones, leaves Enniskillen, hauled by PPs class 4-4-0 No 73.** Neil Sprinks.

This page: **Great Northern lines in the 1950s offered tremendous contrasts, as the views on these first two pages confirm. Dick, the horse which hauled the Fintona horse tram, (see also page 109), is clearly not very interested in Ps class 4-4-0 No 105 arriving with a train from Omagh.** Ian Allan Library.

Opposite page: **A set of 1950s-built AEC railcars are seen outside Foyle Road station in Derry on 24th May 1953.** Neil Sprinks.

CONTENTS

FOREWORD

The root of this strange passion for railways which infuses so many of us has long intrigued me. Perhaps we carry a rogue gene which science has yet to identify, an 'R' gene, possibly modified according to its variants as the GWR, LNER or in this instance, the GNR, not forgetting the (I), gene. This totally unscientific observation is backed by the fact that my brother has a less intense variation of the 'R' gene though sadly, in the case of my children, it seems to have skipped a generation.

My interest in railways goes as far back as my memory and because I was born and raised in Great Northern territory, it was focused on that fine railway. From my push-chair, I persuaded my long-suffering mother to wheel me round the corner on her shopping trips down Market Street in Omagh, to watch the engine shunting at the town's second goods depot at the Market Yard. I recall with total clarity my first venture onto the footplate of a steam locomotive, supervised by my father, on a wet winter's evening at Omagh station. I retain to this day, over forty years after the event, the image of the bright orange glow of the fire combining with the dim platform lights, reflecting on the blue paint of the locomotive. I can even recall the shape of the cab, and even though I did not know this at the time, I would now venture to suggest that I had visited the footplate of one of the early batch of U class 4-4-0s which dated from 1915.

Today, living in a world which is so dependent on the car and the truck for its transport needs, it can be difficult to appreciate just what a pivotal role the railways played in the lives of our fathers and grandfathers. For journeys of any distance, the train was used and a large proportion of goods also came and went on the railways. In the 1950s, much of the economic life of a small provincial town, like the one I grew up in, was regulated by the comings and goings of the trains at the station. To give but a few examples, fresh bread from the big city bakeries came by train, cattle were shipped to the east coast ports and coal for both domestic hearths and the local gasworks arrived at the station. Carters based there collected goods and parcels off the trains and trundled them round the town. Even the cans of films bringing the latest wonders from the fantasy factories of Hollywood or Ealing to the local cinemas, made their local entrance on a porter's barrow at the station.

The railway was an essential part of the local community. The station master was a figure of prominence in the town perhaps not quite on a par with the doctor, priest or minister, but not far below them in the social scale. The labour-intensive steam railway also had the effect of stiffening the local economy by providing steady, if not well paid employment, for a considerable number of people. Many families have a railway connection in their recent histories. In a time of economic uncertainty and emigration in Ireland, north and south, a job on the railway was a base from which a family could flourish. It is not fanciful to suggest that the security which a job on the railway brought and the promise of some sort of pension when you retired, could provide the stability which enabled children to stay on at school and better themselves, in the classic Victorian model. How many of today's upwardly mobile can trace the beginnings of their ascent to a shunter, a guard or a driver on the railway?

Allow me to indulge myself with a bit more nostalgia before I get down to the serious task in hand. Before exploring *the* Great Northern,

let me share with you a few fragments of *my* Great Northern.

Surely the best way to enter the city of Belfast was from the concourse of the original Great Victoria Street station. From the relative tranquillity of the train and the station a few steps and we country fellows were suddenly confronted by the bustle of the city with its procession of great red and cream double deckers, what seemed like an endless flow of traffic and the distinctive nasal voices of the locals, especially the news vendors. My brother still winces with embarrassment when he recalls a trip to the city with parents and me in tow, made in order to make arrangements for his further education at college in Belfast. His attempts to establish some sort of what would now be called 'street cred' were torpedoed as we walked out of the station, by my howls of delight at seeing double decker buses for the first time.

The journey from Omagh up to the city was a vivid experience for a youngster. There was such a stark contrast between the rough farmland of Tyrone and the manicured lawns of the Lagan Valley that they could have been on different planets. I was absolutely petrified by the tunnel at Dungannon the first time I travelled through it. Perhaps I had been asleep at that point on previous trips, but the shock of passing from sunlight into blackness in an instant had such a profound effect on me that I have been told that I closed my eyes and hid under a coat from virtually the end of the platforms at Great Victoria Street on the return trip, until we were safely through the tunnel. Most trains off the GNR Derry Road, as the line from Portadown Junction to Derry was always known in railway circles, stopped at stations up to Portadown but from there they usually ran non-stop to Belfast. To this day, born out of those journeys, I still have a slightly supercilious attitude to the fine town of Lurgan and to Lisburn, which has now been given city status, through whose stations we careered at seemingly breakneck speed.

Of course Omagh was a junction station and up to the closures of 1957, it also saw trains to Enniskillen, Dundalk and Bundoran. The latter destination is still embedded in the folklore of the town. Until relatively recent times, Northern Ireland was 'dry' on a Sunday. Such Presbyterian reticence was not the case south of the border and the summer Sunday excursions which the GNR ran to Bundoran provided the opportunity for families to take the sea air and for other citizens of Omagh, in search of the liquid refreshment denied to them at home, to slake their thirsts. It was said that some Omagh men never got beyond the pubs on Railway Road and were heard to express surprise when told that Bundoran was on the coast. One of my earliest memories, and I cannot have been more than four at the time, is of a man, unsteady on his feet, singing in an open carriage, probably part of one of the AEC diesel units, on the way back from Bundoran. You can guess where he spent his Sunday afternoon!

This cross border line took on its own importance during the Second World War. Many things rationed in the north were freely available in the south and smuggling, always an attractive proposition since the partition of Ireland in the 1920s, now became even more important. The GNR ran special trains out of season during the war, whose unwritten purpose was to enable northerners to stock up on tea, sugar, butter and other essentials which were subject to strict rationing in the United Kingdom. Some passengers would be searched and have their contraband confiscated at the border, but the majority would get through unscathed. Those of us, of a certain age, still remember with distaste, those officious and arbitrary customs men who operated on both sides of the border for the two separate jurisdictions but who clearly graduated from the same faculty of arrogance and unpleasantness. Whatever its manifest failings in other areas, one can only salute the European Union for banishing such amoeba from borders across the continent.

The closure of the Bundoran line probably caused more concern in Omagh than the Suez crisis of the previous year. I remember packing a bag to travel on the last train, but did not get anywhere near it of course. This was the unthinkable or the previously unimaginable actually happening, and it threw all the traffic of the county of Fermanagh and large parts of Tyrone onto inadequate roads. A huge part of the north of Ireland lost its railway services at a stroke and it seemed that suddenly the railway was no longer the permanent and always reliable mode of transport it had appeared to be. It was as if a bond was broken. Before then, those whom one recalls as having cars were the exception, but by the early 1960s, more and more people were turning to the roads, ourselves included. We were all told that the roads would be improved to make up for the loss of

the railways but parts of the Omagh to Enniskillen road today show little improvement from the 1960s.

Politics also played its tawdry part in the demise of the Great Northern. The southern government, which claimed jurisdiction over the northern counties served by the lines closed in 1957, could have continued to subsidise the services on these admittedly loss making routes. Political rhetoric is cheap however, whilst putting some money into loss making railway lines is not, so they did nothing and the legacy of their inaction is a huge gap in the railway map of Ireland.

The first railway age was coming to an end. The citizens of Tyrone, Fermanagh, Monaghan, Armagh and Cavan who lost their lines in 1957 were among the first of many communities across these islands who were to suffer this fate in the next two decades before sanity was restored to public policy and railways were seen as a vital component in a balanced transport strategy and not a relic of the past.

But what of this railway that played such a large part in so many lives and that is still held in great affection today many decades after its demise? I aspire in these pages, to try to recreate something of the spirit of the Great Northern in words and pictures, partly to remind myself what we have lost. In sharing this with others, I hope I may shed a small beam of light on the social and economic history of the north of Ireland in the last decades when the traditional 'Victorian' railway held sway, defining this period as the years from the end of the Second World War to the effective end of steam power on the former Great Northern main line, in 1965, though we shall stray out of these chronological parameters from time to time. However, before getting to that, let us set the scene by giving a brief history of the Great Northern and its antecedents for those who may not be that familiar with the subject.

INTRODUCTION

The origins of what was to become the GNR can be traced back to events which occurred in 1835. In April of that year Thomas Brodigan, a landowner from near Drogheda, published a pamphlet urging the establishment of a railroad (a term often used in this early period of railway history and later appropriated by our cousins across the Atlantic) between Dublin and Drogheda. In August of that year a provisional committee met in Dublin to pursue the scheme. Things were also stirring in Ulster. An article in the Belfast newspaper the *Northern Whig,* on 9th November 1835, under the prophetic heading 'Great Northern Irish Railway', announced that plans were afoot which would lead to the presentation of a bill during the next session of parliament to establish a railway from Belfast through Lisburn, Moira, Lurgan and Portadown to Armagh, with a view to extending it ultimately to the west coast. A committee was set up at a meeting in Belfast on 6th November to seek an Act of Parliament to build a railway from Belfast to Armagh. When the prospectus was published in December 1835, a new name was adopted: the Ulster Railway Company.

On the face of it, both ends of a Dublin to Belfast railway were now being promoted but for those behind the UR, the link to the south was never the priority. For them the main target was always a railway to Armagh and beyond and this reflects the now almost forgotten state of the north of Ireland before the Great Famine. It emphasised the development of the province of Ulster, in the previous 50 to 80 years, as a distinct economic unit. The railway would direct the wealth of the province and its agricultural surpluses into the warehouses of the Belfast merchants. It took 13 years to achieve the original aim of the 1835 promoters and open a railway as far as Armagh. As a symbol of how much had changed in the intervening period, among the traffic in 1848 were trains conveying imported corn to provide relief to famine victims in the west.

Though the connection to Dublin was not the priority of the Belfast promoters, it was inevitable that this would come about in due course, and the origin of Ireland's singular gauge of 5ft 3in came out of this.

In the mid 1830s the British government woke up to the fact that competing gauges in England spelt trouble for the future development of the country's railway network and determined that this should be avoided, as far as Ireland was concerned where railway promotion was still in its infancy with only the short Dublin & Kingstown, built to a gauge of 4ft 8½in, open for traffic. To this end the government established a commission of inquiry which was to set out a plan for future railway development in Ireland and recommend the best gauge for the these lines.

The Irish Railway Commissioners reported in the summer of 1838. Their magnificent report offers a comprehensive picture of economic and social life in Ireland before the Great Famine, for their brief was not just to determine the gauge for Ireland's railways, but to create a blueprint for a national network, and to do this, they had to understand the economy of the country. In relation to the question of the gauge to which their railways were to be built, the commissioners consulted widely, seeking the opinions of what would nowadays be called the great and the good, those who had knowledge and experience of the subject. They took opinions from the opposing camps in England, those advocating Brunel's 7ft broad gauge and the supporters of the narrower gauge of 4ft 8½in. The commissioners came up with a gauge of 6ft 2in as a uniform gauge for Ireland's railways and this was adopted by the UR directors in September 1838.

The UR opened the first section of its line to Lisburn on 12th August 1839 and work soon got under way to extend the 6ft 2in gauge tracks to Lurgan, to which trains ran from 8th November 1841, and to a temporary station at Seagoe, just outside Portadown, in January 1842.

As the UR strode westwards, the progress further south of the Dublin & Drogheda Railway was rather less impressive. Frenzied railway speculation in the years 1836 to 1838 centred on the best route for a line linking Dublin to Belfast. There were two opposing camps: one favouring a coastal route, similar to that eventually built, the other promoting an inland line through Navan and Armagh. These distractions coupled with adverse economic conditions and a reluctance to build anything until the railway commissioners had reported, held up the D&D. By 1842, after further delays involving finance, engineers and contractors, the whole of the line from Dublin to Drogheda had been let to contract and work commenced from the Dublin end. However, reports reached the UR board in late 1842 that the D&D had decided, on the recommendation of its engineer, John (later Sir John) Macneill, to ignore the gauge advocated by the commissioners of the 1830s, and build its line to a gauge of 5ft 2in. This would mean a break of gauge on future journeys from Dublin to Belfast, the very thing the government had hoped to avoid when it established the commission.

The arguments began immediately and involved not only the two companies but the role of the government in regulating the railways through the Board of Trade. The D&D had blatantly disregarded the commissioners' 1838 recommendation and early in 1843 Major General Pasley of the Board of Trade was instructed to examine the reasons which had induced the D&D to do this. He did not take long in his deliberations and in March 1843 he suggested that another inch should be added to Macneill's gauge and that 5ft 3in should be the gauge adopted by the D&D. The directors of the southern company resolved to 'cheerfully adopt' Pasley's gauge but the decision was greeted with disbelief in Belfast. Accusations of bias were made and it was suggested that Pasley has only consulted engineers who favoured the 4ft 8½in gauge in Britain and that Brunel and the advocates of a wider gauge had been ignored. There was anger in the UR camp that an untried gauge was being proposed when the evidence on the ground was that 6ft 2in worked and was perfectly safe and efficient.

Left: **This was the hub of my GNR. In the last summer of the Derry Road, on 29th May 1964, S class 4-4-0 No 171 *Slieve Gullion*, leaves Omagh with a train for Derry. In 1963, No 171, along with her sisters Nos 170 and 174 and VS class No 207, were bought as a stopgap by the UTA from CIE. This quartet retained the blue livery until withdrawal and helped to keep the spirit of the old company alive for a little bit longer.** John Dewing.

Top right: **Today with virtually all freight in the north of Ireland conveyed on the roads, it is easy to forget that there once was an alternative, that provided by the goods trains of the GNR. On 2nd June 1954, QLG class 0-6-0 No 158 leaves Enniskillen with a goods train train for Omagh.** Neil Sprinks.

Below right: **GNR steam locomotives were hard at work on goods trains over the steep banks of the main line into the 1960s. 'Big D', SG3 class 0-6-0, UTA No 35, (GNR No 41) has just passed Cloughoge chapel outside Newry, and is not far from the summit of the line at milepost 65½, as it heads a goods train bound for Dundalk.** Jack Patience.

The D&D opened for traffic, on 5ft 3in gauge tracks, in May 1844. There was no immediate problem as the two lines were still separated by many miles but railway speculation was again gathering pace and this highlighted another aspect of General Pasley's decision. The government realised that if the UR was ultimately forced to conform to the new standard gauge, it would have to be compensated so in 1845, when Acts of Parliament were granted to other railway companies in the north of Ireland, clauses were inserted that these lines were to be built to the 5ft 3in gauge and that these companies should contribute to the expense incurred by the UR when it regauged its route.

Out of the speculation of the mid 1840s came a number of other companies whose lines eventually became part of the Great Northern. The most important of these was the Dublin & Belfast Junction Railway whose aim was to build a connection between the D&D and the UR and complete the Belfast to Dublin route. Other companies subject to these clauses compensating the UR were the Newry & Enniskillen and the Dundalk & Enniskillen. It was not until 1851 and 1853 respectively that the UR was able to extract compensation from these impecunious concerns. The UR itself began to change its gauge in 1845 and by the end of 1847, the entire traffic of the railway was being conveyed on the 5ft 3in gauge. The UR's extension to Armagh, under construction since 1846, was 5ft 3in from the outset, finally opening on 1st March 1848.

The speculation of 1844/45 produced a myriad of schemes many of which were simply mad such as the Kilrush, Dublin & Belfast Junction Railway which hoped to raise £1.5 million to link the small port of Kilrush on the Shannon estuary with the country's two largest cities. However, some of the lines projected were later built and were to form part of the Great Northern. One of these was the Londonderry & Enniskillen, first projected in the 1830s and revived in June 1844. This company reached Omagh in 1852 and Enniskillen in 1854. In 1847 the Portadown & Dungannon, which had the blessing of the UR, was authorised, but did

not reach the latter place until 1858. Renamed the Portadown, Dungannon & Omagh Railway, nominally independent but leased to the UR, it finally completed the route which would later be known as the GNR's Derry Road, in 1861.

The UR's own route to the west of the province was extended to Monaghan in 1858 and on to Clones in 1863. A final extension of this line, the Clones & Cavan Extension Railway, was jointly funded by the UR, the D&D, the D&BJR and the Dundalk & Enniskillen, the latter company operating the line.

The arguments about the course of the Belfast to Dublin link were resolved finally when the coastal route triumphed with the authorisation of the D&BJR. When the first viaduct over the Boyne was opened for traffic in 1853, through railway communication between Ireland's two largest cities was possible for the first time. This company also built the branch from Drogheda to Navan but

offloaded it to the D&D when it opened in 1850. The D&D extended this line to Oldcastle in 1863. The D&BJR also worked the branch from Scarva to Banbridge which opened in 1859.

The final major component of what was to become the Great Northern, the Dundalk & Enniskillen, was authorised in 1845. The first section, from Dundalk to Castleblayney, was opened in 1849. Thereafter progress was slow. Clones not being reached until 1858. The construction of the final part of the line to Enniskillen took a further year.

Other lines promoted in the 1840s also later came into the Great Northern fold. Two of these schemes were based in the town of Newry. In 1846 the Newry, Warrenpoint & Rostrevor Railway was sanctioned. The six miles from Newry to Warrenpoint opened on 29th May 1849. The railway never actually reached Rostrevor where the GNR later had an hotel,

Left: **The GNR served both of Ireland's two large cities and many remote rural locations which did not even have stations. As the use of railcars spread, they could stop on request at level crossings across the company's secondary lines. One such place was Rollingford crossing between Carrickmore and Sixmilecross where Q class No 132 is seen with a train for Derry in the summer of 1958.** Drew Donaldson, courtesy W T Scott.

though from 1877 until 1915 a 2ft 10in gauge horse tramway linked Rostrevor to Warrenpoint station.

The story of Newry's other railway would merit a book to itself. Briefly told, the Newry & Enniskillen Railway was sanctioned in 1845 to build a line linking those towns on a circuitous route via Armagh and Clones. At around the same time, the Dundalk & Enniskillen Railway was authorised to connect those towns. The Newry & Enniskillen was to build the Clones to Enniskillen section first; the D&E line from Dundalk would join this route at Clones. However, the N&E ran into financial difficulties and it was not until 7th January 1854 that the short 3½ mile line from Newry to a junction with the D&BJR at Goraghwood was opened. By now the hopes of building a line to Enniskillen had evaporated and, in 1857, the company changed its name to the more realistic Newry & Armagh Railway.

It was not until February 1865 that the company reached Armagh. The 18 miles from Goraghwood to Armagh were among the most awkward in the whole of Ireland to construct involving severe gradients and two tunnels. One of these, Lissummon tunnel at 1,759 yards in length, was the longest in Ireland. As a footnote to the railways centred on Newry, there was no physical connection between the Warrenpoint line and that to Goraghwood and beyond until September 1861 when a ¾ mile line linking the termini of the two companies was built. The NW&R station at Kilmorey Street was abandoned and a new station opened at Dublin Bridge on the connecting line to the N&A station at Edward Street.

The Dundalk & Enniskillen Railway opened the first part of its line to Castleblayney in February 1849. Progress thereafter was painfully slow. Clones was not reached until 1858 and Enniskillen until the following year. There was one branch off this section, the 7½ mile line from Shantonagh Junction near Ballybay, to

Cootehill, which opened in 1860. A new station was built at Enniskillen to accommodate through running onto the Londonderry & Enniskillen Railway which the D&E leased in 1860. The D&E now worked a line from coast to coast across the north west of Ireland, from Dundalk to Derry. In an Act of 1862, it changed its name to the Irish North Western Railway which was a more appropriate title for the undertaking. One final significant line came into the INWR stable in the 1860s. In 1861, the Enniskillen & Bundoran Railway was incorporated to build a 36 mile long branch from the L&E line at Lowtherstown (latterly known as Bundoran Junction) to the seaside town of Bundoran at the southern tip of County Donegal. This line, which opened in June 1866, was worked from the outset by the INWR. In the next half century several attempts were made to make a logical extension of this line along the coast to Sligo. This was never achieved and the section between Bundoran and Sligo interrupted direct railway communication down the whole west coast of Ireland from Derry to Limerick. Bundoran was destined to remain the terminus of a branch which was busy in summer but somnolent for much of the rest of the year. One final line opened in 1863 and worked by the INWR will only be a footnote to our story. This was the Finn Valley Railway from Strabane to Stranorlar. In 1894 this line was regauged to 3ft and became part of the narrow gauge network of the Donegal Railway. This system was jointly acquired by the GNR and the Midland Railway in 1906.

Other gaps in the railway network in the north of Ireland were filled during the 1860s and 70s. As was common across the Irish Sea, the larger companies often expanded their interests by absorbing or at least working other companies' lines, as we have seen in the case of the INWR working the lines to Bundoran and Derry which it did not actually own. The UR leased and worked two lines which joined its

main line at Knockmore Junction near Lisburn. The first of these was the Banbridge, Lisburn & Belfast Railway which opened for traffic in July 1863. Banbridge had earlier been reached by the D&BJR-worked line from Scarva which opened in 1859. The other line from Knockmore Junction was the grandly named Dublin & Antrim Junction Railway which opened its 18½ mile long line from Knockmore to Antrim in November 1871.

In an Act of 1847 which sanctioned the transfer of the Navan branch from the D&BJR to the D&D, provision was made for the Drogheda company to amalgamate with the D&BJR. It took nearly 30 years for this sensible development to come about and led shortly afterwards to the formation of the Great Northern Railway. It was clearly absurd that a train between Dublin and Belfast would travel on tracks owned by three railway companies but whilst the D&D and the D&BJR were keen to amalgamate, there was a marked reluctance on the part of the UR to give up its independence.

The UR was the most prosperous of all the concerns which were to form the Great Northern. In the 1870s it was regularly paying over 7% in dividends to its shareholders. The D&D was not far behind. Its last accounts as an independent company show that its shareholders were getting dividends of 6%. The D&BJR shareholders got the worst deal of the three companies operating the Dublin to Belfast line: in 1869 their dividend was as little as 3⅞%. However, by comparison with those unfortunate enough to have invested in the INWR, D&BJR stockholders were in clover.

The INWR, with its long main line straggling across relatively poor districts, had never been prosperous. The length of time it had taken to build its route from Dundalk to Enniskillen was indicative of the difficulties it had in raising money for its construction. An Act of 1864 enabled it to reorganise its finances but it never approached prosperity and if anything its position was in decline by the 1870s. Its last accounts published in 1875 showed not only that there was no money available to pay dividends to shareholders, but that the railway was running at a loss. Its management and shareholders saw the economies which would occur if it were part of a larger organisation as their only hope of salvation or even survival.

Discussions about a possible amalgamation began in 1868. The UR directors, feeling that their railway would be weakened by linking up with their less affluent neighbours, showed no enthusiasm for the proposal and nothing came of it. In 1873 the powers for amalgamation with the D&BJR which the D&D had in the 1847 Act and which had long ago lapsed, were revived. Negotiations began between the D&D and the D&BJR and in March 1875 they amalgamated as the Northern Railway Company (Ireland).

In January 1876, the INWR joined the new company which renewed negotiations with the UR. These finally came to fruition on 1st April 1876 when the UR joined the company which was given the revised name, the Great Northern Railway (Ireland). The shareholders of the Ulster Railway did as well at the amalgamation as they had done throughout the company's independent existence. Taking the figure of £100 worth of stock as a mean, D&D shareholders got the same value in the new company, D&BJR shareholders got stock valued at £77½ for their £100, whilst the value of INWR shares was slashed to one sixth of their previous nominal price. In contrast, those holding £100 worth of UR stock saw this appreciate to £124½. This reflects both the solidity of UR dividends and the fact that that company needed substantial inducements to amalgamate with

Below: **A part of the GNR much loved by generations of Dubliners was the company's Hill of Howth Tramway which linked Sutton and Howth stations via the summit of the Hill of Howth. On a busy summer's day in the 1950s, three of the original cars dating from 1901 are seen at the summit.** Neil Sprinks.

its apparently weaker southern neighbours.

The newly formed Great Northern faced a myriad of difficulties in integrating the activities of its previously independent component companies and thus achieving the cost savings, the desire for which had driven the process of amalgamation in the first place. The independent companies had had a total of 41 directors; the first board of the GNR had 29 . There were four engineers and four locomotive superintendents at the start. The largest of the five loco works inherited by the GNR were those of the UR in Belfast. These were controlled by the forceful John Eaton, the UR locomotive superintendent. Ex-UR engines were not renumbered or even reliveried until Eaton retired in 1885.

Shortly after the amalgamation, the decision was made to build a new works at Dundalk. Construction began in 1879 and James C Park, from the English Great Northern Railway, was appointed to run the new works and the railway's locomotive department, though as noted above, Eaton's fief in Belfast did not come under his control until 1885. The GNR had inherited around 140 locomotives from its constituents. These included a wide variety of types and wheel arrangements from a multiplicity of builders. In the interests of economy, a rationalisation of this diverse fleet was a necessity as was a policy of standardisation relating to new locomotives. Park laid down the basic principles which were to be followed for the next 70-odd years by the four engineers who succeeded him at Dundalk. Broadly speaking, this meant a predominance of 0-6-0 types for goods work and 4-4-0 classes for passenger trains.

At its formation the GNR owned, leased or worked about 460 route miles of railway. At its fullest extent between 1910 to 1923, the system extended to over 600 route miles. A lot of tidying up in relation to ownership and operating agreements took place in the years following the amalgamation. The line from Banbridge to Scarva was purchased in 1876 as was the Banbridge, Lisburn & Belfast Railway, whose line from Knockmore Junction, near Lisburn, to Banbridge had previously been worked by the UR. The other line which met the GNR main line at that junction, the Dublin & Antrim Junction Railway, previously leased by the UR, was acquired in 1879. The Newry & Armagh Railway also came into the fold in that year. The company which owned the continuation of that line, the Newry, Warrenpoint & Rostrevor, sold out to the GNR in 1885. The L&E retained its independence until 1883 when it was amalgamated with the GNR. The line which branched off the L&E at Bundoran Junction, the Enniskillen, Bundoran & Sligo Railway, became part of the Great Northern in 1897.

The construction of new lines in the 1870s was also largely concerned with tidying up schemes which had been under way at the time of the amalgamation. The Dungannon & Cookstown Railway, which had been incorporated in 1874 under the auspices of the UR, was opened in 1879. The Banbridge Extension Railway, authorised in the 1860s, to extend the existing line from Knockmore Junction, which went bankrupt in 1865 owing to shortage of funds, was acquired and completed as far as Ballyroney by the GNR in 1880. Much later, in 1906, the GNR extended this line to

Castlewellan where it joined a line from Newcastle built by the Belfast & County Down and opened at the same time. GNR trains had running powers over this section of the BCDR to the popular seaside resort of Newcastle, where the fabled mountains of Mourne swept down to the sea.

Important additions to the railway networks of both Belfast to Dublin were also built at this time. A connection was opened from the GNR main line at East Wall Junction to give the company access to the docks on the north side of the Liffey. This also gave the GNR a connection to the systems of the Great Southern & Western and the Midland Great Western via their lines serving the North Wall.

Back in 1864 a company was floated to build lines connecting the three railways which served Belfast and to construct a central station for the city. The company struggled to raise the capital required and had to abandon the plan for a central station. It did build tramways in Belfast docks giving the railway companies access to this potentially important source of traffic for the first time and a connecting line was built from Central Junction, just outside the UR terminus, to Queen's Bridge via Maysfields. A bridge was also built over the River Lagan to carry a branch which provided a connection to the Belfast & County Down Railway system, at Ballymacarrett Junction.

The Belfast Central Railway ran passenger services from 1875 to 1884 between Central Junction and Queen's Bridge but the growth of street tramways in the city at this time meant that this service was unlikely to be remunerative. The BCR was at the end of its resources and there was only one possible buyer, the GNR, who acquired the company in 1885. The passenger services were ended almost immediately in November 1885 and the line became a useful goods link between the docks, the GNR and the BCDR. Access to the Belfast & Northern Counties system was also possible along quayside tramways beyond the former Queen's Bridge station. The GNR opened a goods depot at Maysfields near the Albert Bridge in 1914 and it was on this site in the 1970s, over 100 years after it was first mooted, that Belfast got its Central station.

At the time of its formation, the main trunks of the GNR network were in place. The number of additional lines built by the company was relatively small and these were mostly branches off existing routes rather than through routes. Some of the first branches added were lines which had been planned many years before their actual execution. When the Clones to Cavan line was being built in the 1860s, authorisation was given in the Act for a branch from Ballyhaise to Belturbet. The INWR did not have the means to build this at that time, but the GNR revived the plan and the branch was finally opened for traffic on 29th June 1885. Two years later the narrow gauge Cavan & Leitrim Railway reached Belturbet from the south, increasing the importance of the GNR branch as an outlet for traffic from the narrow gauge line. In July 1886, the GNR opened a 6½ mile long branch from Inniskeen, between Dundalk and Castleblayney, to Carrickmacross. Ten years later and not far away, in 1896 another branch was opened this time linking the town of Ardee with the GNR Dublin to Belfast line, at Dromin Junction.

The GNR was a strong supporter and guarantor of the City of Dublin Junction Railway which was promoted to build a line linking Amiens Street to the Dublin, Wicklow & Wexford line which terminated at Westland Row station. This important link in Dublin's railway network was finally opened in 1891. On the outskirts of the city an unusual addition was made to the GNR system in 1901 when the company's electric Hill of Howth Tramway was opened. This ran from Sutton station on the Howth branch to the line's terminus, via the Hill of Howth. In March 1906, the opening of the line from Ballyroney to Castlewellan, mentioned earlier, was the penultimate addition to the GNR's portfolio of lines.

Below: **The GNR had access to the dock lines of the Belfast Harbour Commissioners via a tunnel under the Queen's Bridge which had very tight clearances. To get through the tunnel to work these lines, the chimney of A class 0-6-0 No 33, built in 1891, had to be shortened.** Ian Allan Library

The last part of the GNR network to be built was the section from Castleblayney to Armagh. This line was in effect a spoiler to the ambitions of the Midland Great Western Railway to reach northwards into GNR territory. One such effort, a plan to extend that company's branch from Navan Junction to Kingscourt, to Armagh and beyond, was defeated in 1893. In 1899 this plan was revived. Opposed by the GNR, it failed to get parliamentary approval. However, in the horse trading that surrounded this scheme, the GNR gave an indication that it was considering building a line of its own from Armagh to Keady. In 1900 the Kingscourt, Keady & Armagh Railway was promoted. The GNR came to an accommodation with this undertaking which was authorised by parliament in 1902, as the Castleblayney, Keady & Armagh Railway.

Construction began in 1903 and the services from Armagh to Keady commenced on 31st May 1909. The final section from Keady to Castleblayney opened in November 1910. This line is interesting for a number of reasons. Firstly, its origin came out of railway politics rather than from a pressing local transport need, its main purpose being to stop the MGWR expanding into GNR territory. It also harked back in a way to the debates which had been conducted in the 1830s and 40s as to the best route for the Dublin to Belfast line: an inland route or the coastal route which was eventually built. Had the inland route triumphed at that time, its northern section would probably have passed through the district served by the Keady line. The Castleblayney to Armagh line was the last part of the GNR network to be built.

The first decade of the twentieth century saw the GNR at its peak in terms of both its route mileage and its prosperity. In 1906, in partnership with the English Midland Railway, since 1903 the owners of the Belfast & Northern Counties system, the GNR acquired the narrow gauge Donegal Railway. This system was expanded with a new line from Strabane to Letterkenny opening in 1909. Traffic was buoyant across the network. Several stretches of the Derry Road were doubled between 1899 and 1907: those from Portadown Junction to Trew & Moy, Dungannon to Donaghmore and St Johnston to Derry. A new locomotive depot in Belfast was opened in 1911 at Adelaide and a third road was laid to from there to Great Victoria Street. In 1899 the company bought its first hotel and for many decades the Great Northern hotels at Bundoran and Rostrevor were renowned for the quality of their facilities.

The golden age for the GNR and indeed for all the railways of these islands began to wane in August 1914 with the beginning of the Great War. The onset of war brought about a great increase in traffic but also an even greater escalation of costs. The 1916 rebellion in Dublin ushered in a period of dramatic political upheaval for the whole country and its railways. The government took control over all

Irish railways from 1st January 1917. This continued until August 1921, the railway companies being compensated by the government for the arrears of maintenance which had occurred during this period.

Consider some of the changes which took place between 1914 and 1924 and it is easy to see that the GNR and the other Irish railways were now in a radically different world. Firstly, the politics. Whilst the leaders of the 1916 rebellion were largely reviled by the populace at the time of their rebellion, the retribution which followed, the trials and executions, turned much of the public outside Ulster into supporters of independence. Agitation and armed insurrection against British rule in Ireland grew in intensity until 1921 when a political settlement was reached which involved the partition of the country. Six counties of the province of Ulster remained part of the United Kingdom whilst the other 26 counties formed the Irish Free State ruled by a government and parliament in Dublin.

Opposition to the settlement, particularly in the newly created Free State, led to a civil war and an intensification of the violence and mayhem. Attacks on the railways increased during this period, and whilst the GNR was not as badly affected as the lines further south, services were disrupted where signal boxes were set on fire and rolling stock was maliciously derailed. Whilst the physical damage caused further south during the Civil War was eventually made good, for the GNR the long term ramifications of the political turmoil were not so easily resolved.

The company's tracks now crossed an international border in 17 places and the new political reality would in time disrupt the trading patterns which had led to the construction of these lines in the first place. Both passenger and goods trains were subjected to examination by two sets of Customs officials at the designated border crossings and this led to delays and an increase in journey times. One early casualty of the new political geography was the last part of the GNR system to be constructed, the line from Castleblayney to Keady and Armagh which had only been opened throughout in 1910. The section from Castleblayney to Keady had the melancholy distinction of being the first part of the system to close when services were withdrawn in 1923. This line, built at great expense through a sparsely populated district, had been open for less than ten years. Its admittedly modest traffic was disrupted fatally by the imposition of partition.

A major change in the organisation and structure of the Irish railway network also took place at this time. In 1925 all those companies whose lines were wholly within the Free State were forced to amalgamate by the government to form the Great Southern Railways. The lines owned by the Midland Railway in Ulster became part of one of the world's largest railway companies, the London Midland & Scottish Railway, at the grouping of Britain's railways in 1923. Thus in Ireland only the GNR

and a few other minor lines which crossed the border, such as the Sligo, Leitrim & Northern Counties, the Londonderry & Lough Swilly and the County Donegal narrow gauge lines, retained their independence. Being left on one's own in this new world was not necessarily a good thing as the railways were also assailed by adverse economic factors.

The period of the Great War had seen the railway's costs rising sharply. Coal and raw materials had increased in price but perhaps more damaging for the labour-intensive railways was the escalation in wages and the imposition of an eight hour day in 1919, by the Irish Railways Executive Committee, the government body controlling the network in those years. Allied to cost inflation was the first serious threat to the railway's virtual traffic monopoly. In 1914 cars, lorries and buses were rarely seen in Ireland but in the years after the end of the war, a large number of such vehicles, many of them government surplus, entered service. At first there was no regulation of any kind and the new operators competed vigorously with each other and the railways for traffic. In time the governments in Dublin and Belfast passed legislation to regulate these privateers, though in rather different ways.

In the face of the competitive chaos on the roads, in 1927 the two governments passed legislation to allow railway companies to operate road services. The GNR began to buy out private operators and moved towards an integrated system where trains, buses and lorries worked together rather than against each other. In the Free State from 1932 legislation strictly regulated and licensed the activities of those operating bus and lorry services. This helped the GNR, and the GSR, to strengthen their road transport operations and ended the period of unregulated chaos which had preceded this.

In Northern Ireland a rather different approach was applied. An Act of 1935 set up the Northern Ireland Road Transport Board which was delegated to take over all bus and lorry services outside the city of Belfast. The GNR and the other railway companies could no longer operate buses and lorries in Northern Ireland. They had to give up their vehicles to the NIRTB which was supposed to run services in co-ordination with the railways and not in competition with them. In fact this was never done and the buses and lorries of the NIRTB often operated services which competed directly with the railways of the province. The uneasy relationship between the NIRTB and the railways continued into the late 1940s when the Board was replaced by the Ulster Transport Authority. The roots of UTA's policy of antipathy to railways and the primacy of road over rail which it promoted to the detriment of the railways of Northern Ireland can be traced back to the 1930s. In the Free State, the GNR continued to develop its road services and its blue and cream liveried buses were still seen in the border counties of Northern Ireland on services originating in the south.

In many ways, the 1930s was a bleak decade for Ireland, north and south. The economic depression which followed the Wall Street Crash in 1929 quickly spread across the Atlantic. Unemployment greatly increased as economic activity declined. The holders of ordinary shares in the GNR did not get a dividend after 1931 and a bitter railway strike in Northern Ireland in 1933 was marked by two malicious derailments. The strike was a failed attempt to stop wage cuts. This was part of a strategy to control expenditure during these difficult years. Another manifestation of this was the singling of some double track sections. The line between Clones and Armagh was singled between 1932 and 1934 as were parts of the Derry Road, and passenger services between Goraghwood and Armagh were withdrawn in 1933.

However, there were some positive developments in this period. The Boyne viaduct at Drogheda was rebuilt between 1930 and 1932, enabling heavier locomotives to be used on the main line. This led to the introduction of the V class compound 4-4-0s in 1932 and the acceleration of Dublin to Belfast services. The GNR took over the working of the Dundalk, Newry & Greenore line in 1933, a logical move as this outpost of the LMS empire was deep in Great Northern territory.

The 1930s also saw the pioneering development of railcars and railbuses in an effort to reduce the cost of operating passenger services on lightly used lines. This in turn led to the introduction to the timetable of additional halts and stopping places on various parts of the network. The overall financial position of the company declined during the 1930s as expenditure grew and revenue inexorably diminished despite the efforts of a good management team and a loyal workforce. This picture of managed decline was turned on its head following the events of 1939 which led to the start of the Second World War.

When the United Kingdom went to war against Germany in September 1939, the Irish Free State declared itself neutral in the conflict. In both parts of Ireland there were immediate restrictions on the availability of petrol; private motoring was virtually suspended for the duration of the conflict. One consequence of this was that between 1939 and 1943 passenger and goods traffic carried by the GNR virtually doubled. In financial terms the company's revenue increased from £1.3 million in 1938 to £3.4 million in 1944.

In both parts of Ireland most of the traffic lost to the roads since the 1920s was restored to the railways, for the duration of the war, or the Emergency, the name given to the conflict in the Free State. In addition to this, the war brought its own extra traffic to the railways. Northern Ireland became the base for many thousands of Allied troops, as they prepared for the eventual invasion of Europe. There were also a number of air bases in the province and the naval base on the Foyle at Derry played a vital role in the Battle of the Atlantic. All this

concentration of military activity brought much additional traffic to the GNR lines in Northern Ireland. The level of extra traffic south of the border was less intense, though one new traffic flow which grew out of the war was that in turf or peat. The southern government encouraged the production of this indigenous fuel to make up for the shortage of imported coal. The amount of goods carried by the GNR rose from ¾ million tons in 1938 to an astonishing peak of 1¼ tons in 1944. Holders of ordinary shares saw their dividends return between 1941 and 1947.

The restoration of the GNR's prosperity was due to the exceptional conditions which prevailed during the war and it could not be sustained as economic conditions began to return to normal. The pre-war realities of railway economics also began once again to catch up with revenues. There was a certain degree of investment in the system in these years manifested in new steam locomotives and a fleet of modern diesel railcars but this could not be sustained. In 1947 a new and since revered name entered the annals of Irish railway history. On 11th August of that year a new non-stop service between Belfast and Dublin ran for the first time. Called the 'Enterprise Express', a name which is still used for services on the main line over half a century later, this is also a term which could be readily applied to the GNR itself, enterprising and progressive despite the difficult conditions under which it had to operate since the 1920s.

By 1949 the GNR was making losses and in 1950 the board announced that the company had reached the end of its resources and the whole system would have to close. Neither government could countenance this happening so they agreed to finance the company's losses in the short term until a permanent solution could be found. In an example of co-operation rare in those times of frosty official cross border relations, the two governments agreed in 1951 to buy the GNR for £4.5 million. Legislation was passed in both parliaments to create the Great Northern Railway Board which was to run the railway on behalf of both governments. The GNRB consisted of five members appointed by each jurisdiction. It came into being in September 1953 and carried the ethos of the old company on for another five years before it was disbanded and the remaining lines and assets of the GNR were nationalised and divided between the two governments in 1958.

Those few years in the 1950s provided an Indian summer for the spirit of the GNR. But winter follows summer and for the GNR system that fell with a vengeance in September 1957. The responsibility for the destruction of the GNR network must be firmly pinned on the government of Northern Ireland. The reasons for their action were twofold. Since the formation of the NIRTB in 1935, transport policy in the province favoured road before rail. When the UTA was formed in 1948 and took over the BCDR and NCC lines in the

province as well as the road services of the NIRTB, among its first acts was a major programme of railway closures which included most of the BCDR system and a large part of the former NCC system. When busmen are allowed to run a railway, the consequences for the railway can be dire, a sentiment which many unfortunate passengers, sorry, customers, on parts of the privatised British railway network will appreciate.

Allied to this long-standing antipathy to railways was the fact that the GNR was a cross border concern. Many Unionist politicians in Ulster, reflecting the views of their constituents, had little interest in anything outside their own province. It was as if, in their minds, the rest of the island did not exist. There was little cultural affinity with the rest of Ireland and many never travelled across the border. This insularity was not helped by the public conduct of the southern state, neutral during a war that threatened the very existence of Britain, perceived in the north as favouring the views of the dominant religion and also claiming in its constitution jurisdiction over Northern Ireland. Subsidy for a railway which provided as much, if not more, benefit for the Republic was therefore not likely to find much support among the governing class in Northern Ireland.

The GNRB realised that the system had to be modernised if it was to stand any chance of survival and the Board produced plans for many additional diesel railcars and new diesel locomotives. However, it took the two governments a long time to decide anything and only a small part of the Board's proposals, those for new railcars, were sanctioned. In the meantime the railway's staff had to struggle on with worn out equipment which cost a lot to operate and maintain. In the early years of the Board, some closures occurred. The lines serving Banbridge from Scarva and Knockmore Junction were closed in 1955 and 1956 respectively as was the last remaining part of the old Newry & Armagh Railway, that from Goraghwood to Markethill, when its goods service was ended in 1955.

The crunch came in 1956 when the Northern Ireland Ministry of Commerce issued proposals to close all the sections of the former Irish North lines within its jurisdiction and the former UR main line from Portadown through Armagh to Tynan; in other words, up to the border. The remaining sections of these lines in the Republic would be rendered meaningless if the connections through Northern Ireland were closed. The proposals were referred to tribunals on either side of the border which the legislation setting up the GNRB had allowed for. Everyone who gave evidence was opposed to the closures but the Northern Ireland body endorsed the closures whilst that in the Republic opposed them. The Northern Ireland government had no intention of backing down and the closure for these lines was confirmed for the end of September 1957. The legislation setting up the

GNRB allowed either government to continue to run and subsidise services in the other's jurisdiction in the event of a unilateral closure decision such as this. The southern government declined to do this and instead allowed the heart to be ripped out of the railway network of the north of Ireland. Some residual goods and parcels services were continued for a few years on the rump of these lines in the Republic but these were withdrawn by 1960.

The GNRB continued in existence until 1958 when it was dissolved and its assets were equally divided between the two governments. The remaining GNR lines came under the control of the nationalised railway undertakings, the UTA in the north and CIE in the Republic. The closures continued and in 1965 the Derry Road and the lines to Newry and Warrenpoint were condemned, leaving the Knockmore Junction to Antrim line, the Dublin to Belfast route and the branches off this in the Republic as the sole remaining parts of the Great Northern to survive.

In the summer of 2003, the Knockmore to Antrim line lost its sparse passenger service again and was mothballed. Of the over 600 route miles of track once operated by the GNR,

Below: **On 18th May 1960, UTA No 64 (GNR No 196)** *Lough Gill*, **pauses at Aldergrove with a train from Great Victoria Street to Antrim. As noted above, this line is now once again closed to scheduled passenger trains.** John Dewing.

today only the Belfast to Dublin main line and the Howth branch still has passenger trains.

In the pages which follow, I will try not to dwell on the closures and the disgraceful way the company and its staff were betrayed in the 1950s and 60s. Rather, I will focus on the achievements of the GNR, particularly in its later years which many still fondly remember. The company had a long run, from 1876 to 1958 and in those years as well as providing safe and reliable trains for a large part of the north of Ireland, it earned the respect and admiration of those who used those services and lodged itself in the affection of those who study and admire railways. If this book celebrates the legacy of the GNR in a positive way and sheds an affectionate light on a vanished era, then it will have achieved its purpose.

ACKNOWLEDGEMENTS

So many have helped me in the course of this project, that I have not the space to acknowledge them all individually. The photographs are the most important component of this book and I am indebted to the photographers whose work appears in these pages, many acknowledged, others unknown. I am grateful for the access provided to the archives of Ian Allan Publishing where I found many interesting pictures. Thanks are also due to the officers of the Stephenson Locomotive Society for permission to explore their photographic archives. Des Fitzgerald was most helpful in finding views of subjects which I could not find elsewhere and I am grateful to W T Scott for permission to use some of the photos taken by the late Drew Donaldson.

Many friends and colleagues have read parts of the text and given freely of their expertise to attempt to make it fit for human consumption. Particular thanks are due to Derek Russell Hill for his observations on the section dealing with GNR steam locomotives and to Harry Mulholland for information relating to the signalling arrangements at Knockmore Junction. Chris Aspinwall corrected part of the Derry Road chapter and Pearse McKeown, who began his career at Dundalk works, provided much assistance on matters pertaining to the GNR works and the Irish North. Though many have tried to keep me on the right track, if what follows gets derailed in places, despite their best efforts, it is me alone who should have to face the Station Master.

Finally, I would like to dedicate this book to two very good friends, based at either end of the GNR main line, who have given me great help and encouragement in the course of the various projects in which I have been involved over the years: Des McGlynn and Derek Young.

Tom Ferris
Shrewsbury
September 2003

STEAM AND DIESEL TRACTION

Before we begin our travels along the highways and byways of the GNR, let us look at the steam locomotives and other types of motive power which the railway was using during the period which is the focus for this book, the years from 1945 to 1965.

One of the attractions of the GNR, in the early part of this period at least, was the incredible mixture of ancient and modern motive power which could be seen around the system. Strictly speaking, the Great Northern operated four forms of traction up to 1957: steam, diesel, electric and horsepower. As the role played by kilowatts and carrots was fairly marginal and will be covered later in the book, in this chapter we will concentrate on steam and diesel traction.

The development of GNR steam power will be covered in roughly chronological order starting with the oldest steam locomotives which were still in service in late 1940s and ending with the company's last new steam engines, which were delivered in 1948.

This is a story of evolution rather than revolution. Only five men held the job of Chief Mechanical Engineer at Dundalk between 1880 and 1948. Each built on the achievements of his predecessor. The basic types of steam locomotives needed had been established by the turn of the twentieth century, 4-4-0s for passenger trains and 0-6-0s for goods traffic, though the locomotives built to these wheel arrangements were enlarged and improved over the years to match the requirements of the traffic.

In terms of the bigger picture of the railway history of these islands, the contribution made by the GNR to the application of diesel traction to railways is perhaps sometimes overlooked. From the first experiments with railcars in the 1930s to the complete modern diesel trains introduced in 1950, the GNR was a pioneer of this form of traction, which we all take for granted these days.

Left: **When J C Park took charge of the new works at Dundalk in 1880 he was faced with a bewildering array of locomotives, perhaps as many as 50 different designs, inherited from the companies which had amalgamated to form the GNR. His principal task was to begin a process of standardisation to impose some order on this chaos. The first engines to enter service under his stewardship were the four H class 2-4-0s dating from 1880/81. No 87, built by Beyer Peacock in 1880, was withdrawn in 1931 but is included here to represent this first phase of GNR locomotive design. Though the type was based on an older D&BJR design, visits to Dundalk works over the years have added many standard GNR features such as the cab, chimney and tender.** Ian Allan Library.

Left: **Most of the locomotives inherited from the constituent companies had been scrapped by the turn of the last century as new and more powerful GNR designs became available. One of the last survivors was 4-4-0T No 196, built by Beyer Peacock in 1880 for the Belfast Central Railway. The locomotive was latterly used for shunting at Dundalk and is seen at Barrack Street goods yard there on 29th August 1947. The engine was scrapped in 1950.** John Dewing.

Top left: **Park's first new design was the A class 0-6-0 of which 15 were built between 1882 and 1891. No 60, seen here at Enniskillen shed, emerged from Dundalk works in 1890 and was withdrawn by CIE in 1959. All of the class were later rebuilt to conform to the specification of the later AL class locos, but these were the first in a long line of 0-6-0s which were to handle the company's goods traffic throughout its existence. Writers on locomotive affairs have noted the stylistic similarities between the locos of the two Great Northerns which Park brought with him across the Irish Sea from his former employers. These characteristics were first noted in the building of these locomotives. Incidentally, the letter A above the number (similar letters will be noted on the cab sides of other 0-6-0s throughout the book) is not a reference to the class of the locomotive, No 60 had been rebuilt as an AL by this stage anyway. Rather it relates to the haulage capacity of the engines.**
Ian Allan Library.

Centre: **As mentioned above, the A class 0-6-0s were followed by the heavier and more powerful AL class engines of which 11 were built between 1893 and 1896. No 32, seen at Enniskillen shed, was built at Dundalk in 1894 and was withdrawn by the UTA in 1960. Up to the time of the Great War most GNR locomotives, even humble goods engines, had names. During these years No 32 was named *Drogheda*.**
Ian Allan Library.

Bottom left: **The pattern for GNR goods engines for the next half century was established by Park with the A and AL classes. Up to this time the usual wheel arrangement for passenger locos was the 2-4-0, as epitomised by No 87 and her sisters. A pair of 4-2-2s, the only ones ever to run in Ireland, introduced in 1885, were followed by the first of the GNR 4-4-0 designs, a wheel arrangement which was perpetuated up to 1948 for the company's passenger engines. The first GNR 4-4-0s, Park's J class, 12 engines built between 1885 and 1889, were also his least successful. All had been withdrawn by 1924 long before our period. However, these were followed by two classes of 4-4-0 some of which lasted into the 1960s, the famous P class. Two variants of the type, built with differing sizes of driving wheels, were introduced in 1892. Between 1892 and 1895 four locos with 6ft 7in drivers were built; the 8 locos with 5ft 6in wheels were spread over the years 1892-1906. No 88, seen at Enniskillen station, represents the locos with the smaller wheels. Dating from 1904, she was withdrawn in 1956.**
Ian Allan Library.

Left: **No 26 represents the variant of the P class with the 6ft 7in driving wheels. Built by Beyer Peacock in 1892 as No 83, this locomotive was renumbered 26 in 1931 when she was also superheated, this changing her designation to Ps class. The larger splashers required for the bigger driving wheels distinguish this version of the P class. No 26 is seen here at Ballyhaise with the 11.45am Cavan to Clones train on 11th May 1956.** SLS collection.

Left: **Park died in May 1895 and was succeeded by Charles Clifford, who had joined the INWR back in 1861. He remained in charge at Dundalk until 1912 during which time he introduced some outstanding engines. Clifford's first design introduces another characteristic GNR practice. The company believed in standardisation and in terms of the locomotives this meant that contemporary passenger and goods types shared many parts, notably boilers. Whilst Park's J class 4-4-0s were not very successful, all six JT class 2-4-2 tank engines, which used some of their parts, lasted into the 1950s. Often seen on the branch from Ballyhaise to Belturbet, No 92 is at the terminus on 13th June 1949. After years of dereliction, this attractive GNR station with its train shed has been lovingly restored by local people.** Ian Allan Library.

Below: **The JT tanks really owed much to his predecessor even though they were introduced at the start of Clifford's stewardship at Dundalk. The new engineer's first original design was the PP class 4-4-0s of which 17 were built between 1896 and 1911. These had driving wheels 6ft 7in in diameter, a size used in all subsequent GNR 4-4-0s. The PP class locomotives were later rebuilt with superheated boilers, changing their designation to PPs, the last letter denoting the change. No 107 was built by Beyer Peacock in 1906 and rebuilt with a superheated boiler in 1929. In this side view taken at Enniskillen shed, which emphasises the size of the driving wheels, the locomotives is spotlessly clean. No 107 was withdrawn by the UTA in 1958 after over 50 year's service.** Ian Allan Library.

Right: **The next new class was the PG 0-6-0, of which seven were built between 1899 and 1904. Given their designation, it might be thought that they had much in common with the earlier P class 4-4-0s. In fact they were really a development of Park's AL class. The complete class went to the UTA in 1958. No 100 which lasted until 1961, is seen here shunting coaching stock at Great Victoria Street station in Belfast on 23rd June 1937.** H C Casserley.

Below right: **This is where it gets a bit complicated; enter the Q family. The earlier GNR 4-4-0s had been fairly underpowered, ideal for working secondary routes where they had long and active lives, but inadequate for the main lines where trains were getting heavier. Clifford's solution was the Q class, 13 locos built between 1899 and 1904, bigger and more powerful and on a par with the best of similar types at work on the other side of the Irish Sea at the time. Representing the class is No 123 built by the North British Locomotive Company in Glasgow in 1903. This originally carried the diabolical name, *Lucifer*.** Ian Allan Library.

Top: **The Qs were followed by the slightly more powerful QL class 4-4-0s of which eight were constructed between 1904 and 1910. No 128, another North British product dating from 1907, is seen arriving at Amiens Street station in Dublin with a very mixed rake of coaching stock, in the early 1950s.** John Kennedy.

Left: **The Q class passenger engines were shadowed by four types of 0-6-0s. The first of these was the QG class consisting of four locomotives built in 1903/04. These had the same size of cylinders and boiler as the Q class 4-4-0s. North British-built QG No 153 is seen here at Ballybay on a passenger working in this 1930s view.** Ian Allan Library.

Centre left: **The QGs were followed by the LQG class. Introduced in 1906, 11 locos were built in two years. These machines had larger boilers than the QGs. One of the first of these, No 110 built in 1908, another North British product, is seen here at Derry in 1951.** John Edgington.

Bottom: **The final variants were the five NQG class locos of 1911 and No 165, the solitary NLQG engine constructed the same year. All were built by Nasmyth Wilson of Leeds. The numbers of the NQTs were 9, 38, 39, 109 and 112; the NLQG was No 165. No 9, seen at Derry in June 1937, like the others was later superheated. This term which is often bandied about merits explanation. Superheating is a process whereby the steam produced by a boiler is heated a second time to dry it and increase its temperature. Superheated steam is more efficient in generating traction through a loco's cylinders than the 'wet' steam provided by a non-superheated or saturated boiler. The application of superheating was coming into vogue in the years before the Great War. Though superheated boilers were more complicated to make and maintain, the advantages were so manifest that a large numbers of GNR locomotives were fitted with superheated boilers on their visits to Dundalk works over the years for overhaul.** H C Casserley.

Below left: **The GNR was never a big user of tank engines, but there were two tank engines designs in the Q family, evidence of Clifford's espousal of the practice of standardisation. Two QGT 0-6-2Ts, Nos 98 and 99, were built by Robert Stephenson in 1905. A modified version in the form of two QGT2s came from the same firm in 1911. There were minor differences between the two types but visually they were virtually identical. Used for shunting mainly, No 99 is seen at Adelaide shed in Belfast.** H C Casserley.

Below right: **Another Clifford tank engine design was the RT class 0-6-4T, of which four were built by Beyer Peacock between 1908 and 1911, Nos 22, 23, 166 and 167. They were built specifically to work the goods yards and dock lines in Belfast. They had small 4ft 3in driving wheels and a short** wheelbase which enabled them to negotiate the sharp curves on the dock lines. Their cab and boiler mountings were reduced in height as some of the clearances on the lines they worked were very tight, in particular in the short tunnel at the Queen's Bridge in Belfast which gave access to the dock lines. A rather grubby No 22, is seen at Adelaide shed in Belfast. Ian Allan Library.

Bottom: **Charles Clifford retired in 1912 after a career of over 50 years to be succeeded by George Glover who came to Dundalk from the North Eastern Railway in England. Before he retired, Clifford produced a final passenger locomotive design which is regarded by many as his masterpiece. For me, a non-technical man, as impressed by the aesthetics of a locomotive as by its performance, Clifford's** S class 4-4-0s are simply the most beautifully proportioned and elegant machines ever to grace an Irish railway. The eight locos, named after Irish mountains, were superheated from the outset. Fully renewed in the 1930s by Glover, they were superb performers, mostly on the main line and the Derry Road, for nearly half a century. Those of us around today have no recollection of the green livery which they carried when built, but in the later sky blue livery they looked simply stunning, as evidenced by No 191 *Croagh Patrick*, waiting here at Dundalk in June 1954 to whisk the 'Bundoran Express' up to Dublin. One of the class, No 171 *Slieve Gullion*, has been preserved by the Railway Preservation Society of Ireland and continues to perform gallantly in the service of the society on lines the length and breadth of the country. Ian Allan Library.

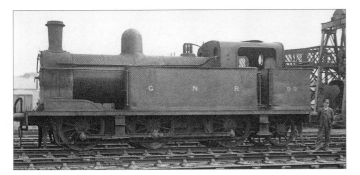

Top left: **In true Great Northern fashion, the new passenger engines were followed by an 0-6-0 variant for goods working, the SG class. The two types had the same cylinders and boilers. The wheel dimension was increased from the 4ft 7¼in of the earlier 0-6-0s, to 5ft 1in in the SGs. The larger wheel size gave them a greater turn of speed and made them suitable for occasional passenger workings. Five SGs were delivered in 1913 and a further 10, the SG2 class, incorporating some modifications made by Glover, were built between 1915 and 1925. SG class No 179, built by Beyer Peacock in 1913, is seen here at Ardee.** Ian Allan Library.

Below: **To complete the S class engines, we have to move ahead to 1920/21 when the penultimate GNR 0-6-0, and certainly the most powerful locomotive of this wheel arrangement to run in Ireland, the SG3 class, arrived on the scene. All 15 engines**

were built by Beyer Peacock. No 118 is seen here on the turntable at Clones shed. The SG3's power classification letter, 'D', is above the number. These engines were affectionately known to railway enthusiasts as the 'Big Ds' to distinguish them from the other locomotives in this power classification. Until the Boyne viaduct at Drogheda on the main line was rebuilt in 1932, the SG3s were deemed too heavy to pass over it. However, they were invaluable in dragging heavy goods trains up the banks north of Dundalk. Ian Allan Library.

Opposite page, bottom: **Having said that the GNR was not a big user of tank engines, Glover's first design, built between 1913 to 1929, the T1 and T2 4-4-2 tanks, were the company's most numerous class. The first five built in 1913 had saturated boilers, but were later rebuilt with superheaters. The remaining 20 engines had superheated boilers from the start. The main outward difference between the two types was in the shape of their cab windows. I have always found them very difficult to tell apart other than by referring to their numbers. They were used mainly on suburban services at either end of the main line. No 4, a T2 class engine built by Beyer Peacock in 1921, and an unidentified sister, are seen at Amiens Street in August 1935.** SLS collection.

This page, centre and bottom right: **Glover's next locomotive was in effect a superheated tender engine version of his 4-4-2 tank. The U class 4-4-0 was a modern light 4-4-0 for the secondary lines. Five were built in 1915 and then 33 years later in 1948, another five were added to the fleet. The later engines had better cabs and modern tenders. The first batch, which entered service during the austere days of the Great War, were unnamed. In the years after the Second World War all the U class were painted in the blue livery and were named. No 197 was given the name *Lough Neagh* in 1949. The different tenders and cabs of the two batches are apparent in these views. No 197 was photographed at Dundalk in May 1949. In the official works photo of No 203 *Armagh*, one of the 1948 locos, the modern tender and the larger cab with side windows, which offered much greater protection to the crew, are apparent.** Both, Ian Allan Library.

Above: **The final type of GNR tank was this one-off 0-6-0 crane tank, No 31, built by Hawthorn Leslie in 1928 for shunting and lifting duties at Dundalk works, where it is seen in this May 1938 view. In the 1950s this locomotive was equipped with a proper coal bunker to extend its limited coal capacity.** SLS collection.

Above: **Almost inevitably, the U class 4-4-0s were accompanied by a 0-6-0 variant. However, the first of these did not appear until 1937, some 22 years after the passenger engines! The first five UG class 0-6-0s were built at Dundalk in that year, the last new engines to be constructed there. A further five were supplied by Beyer Peacock in 1948. The class was designed by George Howden, who had replaced Glover when he retired in 1932. They had the same boilers as the U class 4-4-0s. The UGs were light and powerful and could run anywhere on the system. They were as much at home on passenger trains as on goods workings. The bigger side window cabs, which we saw on the 1948 U class 4-4-0s, first appeared on these machines. Two UGs, GNR numbers 146 and 149, of the 1948 batch, were the last GNR steam locomotives to be withdrawn. They went to the UTA in 1958 who renumbered them 48 and 49. They survived until 1968 by which time they were in the hands of their third owner, Northern Ireland Railways, who took over the province's railways when the UTA was broken up. One of the reasons for their survival was that they were light enough to cross over the fragile Lagan viaduct in Belfast on the line connecting the remaining part of the Belfast & County Down system, the branch from Belfast to Bangor, to the rest of the network. UG No 48 is seen here at Bangor with a train of GNR coaches which had formed an excursion from Portadown to the seaside at Bangor, on 15th July 1964.** Ian Allan Library.

Above left: **This brief résumé of the GNR steam locomotives which were to be seen in the post Second World War era concludes on two high notes: the V class 4-4-0s of 1932 and the VS class of 1948. For years the company had been handicapped by the weak condition of the viaduct over** the Boyne at Drogheda. The work to renew and strengthen the viaduct was completed in 1932, allowing heavier and more powerful locomotives to be used on the Belfast to Dublin main line. To mark this, Glover introduced his five V class compound 4-4-0s in that year. The principle of compounding is simple, the steam the boiler produces is used twice, first in a high pressure cylinder and then further energy is extracted from the same steam in lower pressure cylinders, before it is exhausted through the chimney. Compounds are generally more economical on coal than a simple expansion engine, but the downside is that mechanically they are more complicated and maintenance bills are greater. The GNR compounds were a success and they enabled schedules on the main line to be speeded up. In a reversal of previous policy, the new locomotives were named, after birds of prey, though when they first appeared they were turned out in the then standard black livery. However, in 1936, they were the first GNR locomotives to get the new blue livery which they carried for the rest of their lives. Even the UTA didn't have the nerve to paint them black. The first of the class, No 83 *Eagle*, is seen here at Adelaide in the company of No 57, one of the UTA's WT class 2-6-4 tank locos. This was on loan to the GNR in 1952/53, thus helping to date this photograph. Ian Allan Library.

Opposite page bottom left; **The final GNR steam locomotive design was the VS class which consisted of five locomotives, designed by the company's last locomotive engineer, H R McIntosh, delivered from Beyer Peacock's works in Manchester, in 1948. The company's finances had improved during the war and there was some money available for investment in new equipment, both steam locomotives, and as we will see later, diesel railcars. The VS was a simple or non-compound version of the V class. From this we can assume that, even the though the V class were fine engines, the savings in coal consumption had been negated by the increased maintenance costs which the more complex compound system entailed. The VS class were the heaviest and most powerful of the long line of Great Northern 4-4-0s. Problems with steam drifting down and obscuring the driver's view meant that they were fitted with smoke deflectors in their first year in service, the only class of Irish locos to be so equipped. The VS class were restricted to the main line because of their weight. They were almost certainly the last 4-4-0s built anywhere in the world. No 207 *Boyne* had worked a rugby special from Belfast when recorded at Amiens Street on 7th December 1963. No 207 had gone to CIE in 1958 but was bought by the UTA in 1963 to ease a temporary shortage of motive power.** Derek Young.

Below: **If you were a passenger waiting for a GNR train in the early 1950s, there was perhaps a 50% chance that when your train turned up, it would be powered by diesel rather than steam. The Great Northern was *the* pioneer of diesel traction in the British Isles. The potential for savings brought about by this form of traction was recognised by the company in the 1930s long before this particular penny had dropped elsewhere. The GNR had experience of petrol engined railcars built for the narrow gauge County Donegal Railways, which it jointly owned with the LMS/NCC. The company built the first diesel powered railcars to run in these islands in 1930/31 for the CDR and followed these in 1932 with two diesel railcars for itself. Railcar A had a mechanical transmission whereas with B the diesel engine was used to drive a generator which produced current to feed the electric motors which drove the vehicle. The two pioneering railcars looked very similar. This very early view of Railcar A, taken at the Grosvenor Road goods yard in Belfast, shows the vehicle in its original condition, with the radiator of the AEC engine prominent. When this was later replaced by a Gardner power unit, the radiator was moved to the roof. Railcar B was converted to an unpowered trailer in the 1946 but A soldiered on into the 1960s.** Ian Allan Library.

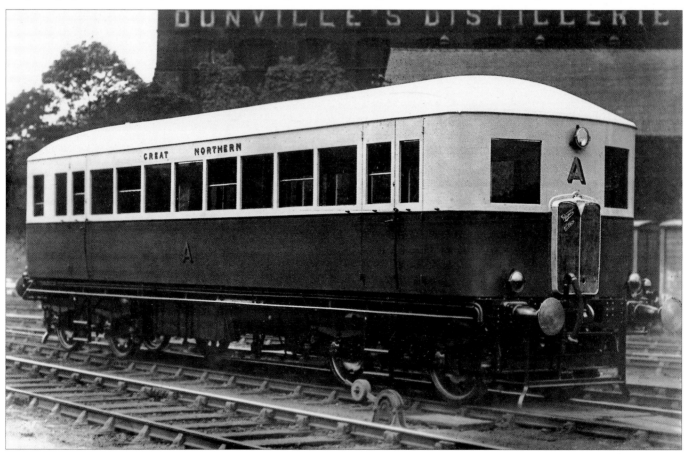

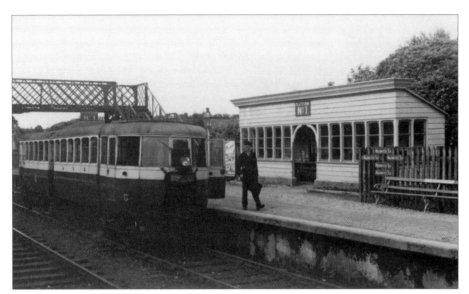

Left: **The next railcar was logically Railcar C, built at Dundalk in 1934. Like the later CDR railcars, the driving compartment containing the engine was articulated from the passenger saloon. Powered by a Gardner diesel engine, unlike A and B, but like the CDR vehicles, C could only be driven from one end and had to be turned at journey's end. On 29th June 1950, C_1 as it was later designated, was recorded at Bundoran Junction on an Omagh to Enniskillen working. This railcar spent much of its time working on the Irish North and we will see it again later on our travels.** John Edgington.

Above: **The next railcars were C_2 and C_3. They were designed to work together back to back as seen here in this view taken at Dundalk in 1935, the year they were built. The engines were not controlled in multiple so one ran as an unpowered trailer when they worked together. They were soon split up and ran as two separate railcars for many years, both lasting into the 1960s.** Ian Allan Library.

Left: **The next railcars, D and E, moved the concept on a bit more. They had a central unit containing the engine which drove six wheels connected by coupling rods, similar to those on a steam locomotive. Two passenger saloons, both with driving positions, were joined to the centre unit. This official photograph of the newly completed Railcar D was taken at Dundalk and appeared in the June 1936 issue of the magazine *Modern Transport*.** Ian Allan Library.

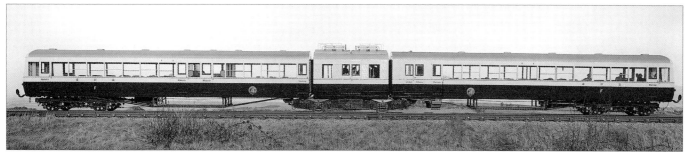

Above: **In 1938, two further railcars, F and G, were introduced. These were an improved version of the previous pair. The six coupled wheels of the centre section were replaced by a four wheel bogie from whose ends the passenger saloons were also pivoted, as this official photograph clearly shows. F and G were powered by two Gardner 6LW diesel engines making them more sprightly than D and E. All the GNR railcars were painted in an attractive blue and cream livery similar to that used on the company's buses. These four railcars seemed to spend a lot of their time working on the Howth branch and on the line to Warrenpoint. Pictorial evidence of their working elsewhere on the GNR system is rare.** Ian Allan Library.

Below: **There is one other aspect of the GNR's embrace of the internal combustion engine which we should not ignore and that was the railbus. This was literally a road bus converted to run on rails by means of the Howden-Meredith patent wheel, the result of a collaboration between two Dundalk engineers and the Dunlop Rubber Company. The wheel combined the use of a steel flanged rail wheel and a pneumatic tyre. The first of these vehicles appeared in 1934. Others were built by the GNR for their impecunious neighbours at Enniskillen, the Sligo, Leitrim & Northern Counties Railway. A railbus offered a most economical way of operating a passenger service on a line where the amount of passenger traffic on offer could not have supported the costs of steam trains.**

Passengers entered the vehicle by means of a platform at the rear which was set at the height of station platforms. Steps were also provided down to rail level which allowed the railbus to pick up passengers at level crossings thus greatly increasing the range of places which could be served without the need for the expense of building stations or halts with conventional platforms. One of the first lines to see the use of railbuses was the branch from Drogheda to Oldcastle and as we can see here, these vehicles were still being used on this branch over 20 years later. Railbus No 1, built in 1934, sits in the down mainline platform at Drogheda on 3rd June 1957, having recently arrived from Oldcastle. F W Shuttleworth.

Opposite page bottom: **The coming of war in 1939 cut short the GNR's development of diesel railcars, but in 1948, with money to invest following the upsurge in traffic during the war, the company ordered 20 railcars from AEC. This firm had been building railcars for the Great Western Railway in England before the war and now had a control system which enabled two power cars to be operated by one driver. The GNR railcars were delivered in 1950 and 1951. Each train consisted of two power cars with a centre trailer. Various combinations were possible, provided the trailers were fitted for working with the power cars. These railcars were seen as the way forward by this progressive and enterprising concern. The GNR at the time the AEC cars entered service was operating the largest and most modern fleet of diesel trains in the British Isles. Four of the sets are seen in this company publicity photo at Great Victoria Street station in Belfast. This was the GNR's vision of the future and was years ahead of its time. The company foresaw the day when virtually all its passenger services would be operated by diesel railcars.** Ian Allan Library.

Opposite page top: **The flexibility of the railcars was such that they could be used for express workings on the main line or on suburban workings like the Howth branch where a four car set, with railcar No 606 nearest the camera, is seen on 27th May 1958. In Ireland, right up to the present day, the term railcar(s) is always used to describe trains which would be referred to as diesel multiple units on the other side of the Irish Sea. Former GNR railcars continued to provide services on the Howth branch into the 1970s. Many were then converted to unpowered trailers fitted with plastic seats. Hauled by CIE C class diesel locomotives, they helped maintain a service of sorts until the line from Howth to Bray was electrified in the 1980s.** John Edgington.

Below: **Apart from a solitary MAK diesel acquired on a trial basis in 1954, the GNR's final flourish with diesel traction came with the BUT cars, the first of which were delivered in 1957. To be precise these 24 powered railcars were ordered by the GNR Board. AEC had become part of the British United Traction Company so, in that** respect, the new vehicles were an evolution from the earlier railcars. Eight vehicles had a driving compartment at one end and a corridor connection at the other. The remaining 16 railcars, such as No 701 seen here, had corridor connections and driving compartments at both ends. This meant that these railcars were very flexible in that they could run in up to eight car formations. Unpowered trailers were converted from existing coaches to run with the BUT cars. The new vehicles were immediately put to work on the prestigious 'Enterprise Express' on the main line between Belfast and Dublin. This usually consisted of an eight coach formation, composed of four power cars and four trailers. Had the GNRB been allowed to continue, and been given the money required to complete its modernisation programme, most passenger services would have been worked by diesel railcars by the end of the 1950s. This would have led to the virtual elimination of steam traction long before this occurred across the Irish Sea. This publicity photograph of No 701 was taken at Dundalk on 15th June 1957.** Ian Allan Library.

THE MAIN LINE
AND ITS BRANCHES

We will begin our photographic journey along the tracks of the Great Northern system with a trip along the main line from Belfast to Dublin. Almost unbelievably, out of a network which at its peak consisted of over 600 route miles of track, at the time of writing, the main line between Ireland's two largest cities and the short branch from Howth Junction to Howth in the Dublin suburbs are the only parts of the former GNR network to retain a passenger service.

Growing up in County Tyrone, the only part of this route I really knew well in steam days was

the section from Portadown Junction to Great Victoria Street in Belfast which was traversed by trains off the Derry Road. It was only when I moved to Belfast in the early 1970s that I really got to know the main line. Maybe I am just a sad old romantic and perhaps my affection for the line is simply because it is all that is left of the GNR, but I think that the 112 or so miles between the two cities offers one of the great rail journeys in these islands. Even in the sanitised air-conditioned, smoke free environment of the current 'Enterprise Express' stock, the landscape which unfolds past the window as the

journey proceeds is so varied that there is always something of interest to see. The line also includes two of the great civil engineering spectaculars of the Irish railway system, the viaducts at Craigmore and Drogheda.

We will begin our journey then in Belfast, at Great Victoria Street station, and head south. In addition to the main line itself, we will explore the branches which fed it, the lines to Antrim, Banbridge and Newcastle, Newry and Warrenpoint and the branches to Ardee, Oldcastle and Howth.

GREAT VICTORIA STREET

Below: **This view, showing the exterior of Great Victoria Street station in Belfast, was taken in 1963. The station, a few** minute's walk from the City Hall and the centre of Belfast, was closed in 1976 when services were diverted to a new station on the site of the GNR's goods yard at Maysfields, a draughty location beside the River Lagan. Laughingly called Belfast Central, this was a bus ride away from anywhere remotely central. Later wiser counsels prevailed and a new station, for suburban services at least, was opened at Great Victoria Street in 1995. The attractive portico has long gone, but at least the convenience of this location has been restored to travellers. *John Langford*

Above: **In this 1937 view, S class 4-4-0 No 191, in original condition, unnamed and in the drab 1930s black livery, arrives at Great Victoria Street on a Dublin service.**

Below: **In 1863 the original level crossing at the station throat over Durham Street was replaced by the so-called Boyne Bridge. This interesting view showing that** bridge's renewal in 1936, also illustrates the station's train sheds. The familiar dome of Belfast City Hall is in the top right of the picture. Both, Ian Allan Library.

Above: **In another classic pre-war view, V class compound No 84 *Falcon*, in its original condition with a round-topped boiler, and sporting the then new blue livery, prepares to leave Great Victoria** Street with a Dublin express. These engines were often referred to by GNR men as 'the pounders'. Ian Allan Library.

Below: **T class 4-4-2 tanks were usually found shuffling round Great Victoria Street on station pilot duties. Here No 187 is seen shunting some vans at the station on 11th June 1960.** Des Fitzgerald.

Top left: **Acting as station pilot at Great Victoria Street on 10th June 1949, was one of the small (5ft 6in) wheeled Ps class 4-4-0s, No 89. When built in 1904, this locomotive and her sister, No 88, took the names *Victoria* and *Albert* and numbers of the two 4-2-2 locomotives, withdrawn that year after short lives, by GNR standards, of only 19 years. No 89 was superheated in 1923, and was withdrawn in 1956.** SLS collection.

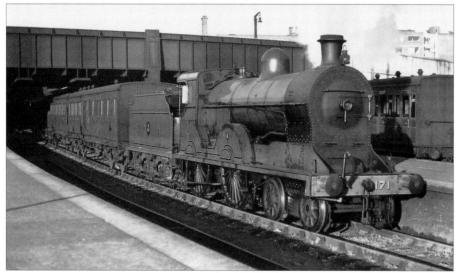

Centre left: **Some locomotives crop up in a large number of photographs whereas other seem to be positively camera shy. In the latter category is one particularly famous GNR survivor, which does not often feature in the photographic record from the days of steam. This is the now preserved S class 4-4-0 No 171 *Slieve Gullion*. In this undated photograph, she is seen at Great Victoria Street with what looks, judging by the non-corridor stock of her train and the one at the adjacent platform, to be an evening suburban working. Both ends of the GNR main line had, by Irish standards, busy suburban services. The company had to fit these in amid long-distance trains.** SLS collection.

Bottom left: **Q class 4-4-0 No 121 is seen at Great Victoria Street in August 1956. The station had four platforms under the roofs of its train shed. There was an additional platform outside the protection of the overall roof, at the south side of the station. This was known as 'the motor platform' from the days when steam railmotors on suburban services to Lisburn had used it. To the left of the picture were the carriage sidings where stock was stored and cleaned. Next to these was the Grosvenor Road goods depot. In 1907/08 a third line was built from the entrance to the goods depot out as far as Balmoral in connection with the opening of the new engine shed at Adelaide. Just beyond the start of the third road was Central Junction where the former Belfast Central Railway line linking the GNR to the BCDR and, via dock lines, to the NCC, branched off the main line.** Ian Allan Library.

THE BELFAST CENTRAL RAILWAY

Top: **The Lagan viaduct, also known as the shaky bridge, carried the BCR line across the river to connect with the BCDR just outside Queen's Quay, at Ballymacarrett Junction. The weak condition of this bridge meant that only the lighter GNR classes were allowed over it. UG class 0-6-0, UTA No 48, the former GNR No 146, brings a return Sunday School excursion from Bangor across the bridge on 20th June 1964.** Des Fitzgerald.

Above: **GNR RT class 0-6-4T No 23 made it across the bridge on 2nd February 1953 and is seen here on BCDR territory, just outside Queen's Quay station.** Neil Sprinks.

Right: **This line also served the GNR's Maysfields goods depot on whose site, beside the Lagan, Belfast Central station was built in the 1970s. With the gasholders of the Ormeau Gas Works behind it, No 23 is seen again, this time shunting at Maysfields on 28th August 1957.** A E Bennett.

Right: **At East Bridge Street Junction, the line to the left of the picture branched off and ran parallel with the river as far as the Queen's Bridge which it passed under in a short tunnel with limited clearances. It then ran onto Donegall Quay, where it made an end-on junction with the Belfast Harbour Commissioners' lines which in turn were linked to the NCC near York Road. UTA buses at Oxford Street bus depot can be seen to the left of the picture.** Desmond Coakham.

Below; **This is the BCR station at Queen's Bridge in August 1957 which had not seen a passenger train since 1885 when the GNR took over the company. Its value since then had been to link the docks to the rest of the city's railways.** A E Bennett.

Left: **On 11th June 1958, GNR A class 0-6-0 No 150 has squeezed under the Queen's Bridge and is seen on the lines north of the bridge, at Donegall Quay. The crew are waiting for a mobile crane behind the locomotive to move and clear the line. Horse-drawn and motor vehicles add to the chaos. The clearances between the locomotive and the line of wagons to the right of the picture are also very tight. These tracks were owned by the Belfast Harbour Commissioners. Incredibly, despite the nature of these lines, the LMS/NCC did operate occasional passenger services onto Donegall Quay to connect with cross channel steamers. One such working is illustrated on page 85 of a companion volume in this series, *The LMS In Ireland*.** John Langford.

ADELAIDE SHED

Top: **Back to the main line, where we will now visit the largest locomotive depot on the Great Northern, at Adelaide less than a mile beyond Central Junction. The shed, which opened in 1911, replacing the earlier Ulster Railway one that was located close to Great Victoria Street station, had nine roads and could accommodate over 50 engines. One oft remarked oddity about Adelaide was that almost incredibly for a shed of its size, it never had a turntable. Engines were turned on a triangle of lines on the site. This classic view, taken from a conveniently sited footbridge, shows S class No 190** *Lugnaquilla*, **SG2 class No 184 and V class compound No 86** *Peregrine*, **outside the main shed.**

The arches in the background carried a line to the coaling stage up which wagons of coal for the locomotives were hauled. A E Bennett.

Above left: **On 21st May 1949, VS class No 206** *Liffey* **is seen at the coaling stage. The locomotive is in its original condition, before smoke deflectors were fitted.** John Dewing.

Above right: **One of the features of Adelaide was an open-air wheel drop. This enabled locomotives to be lifted to allow their wheels to be removed for attention or to provide access to wheel bearings. On 20th June 1956, S class No 173** *Galtee More* **has been lifted to allow the removal of her driving wheels, which can be seen between the locomotive and its tender.** Peter W Gray.

Above: **With the floodlights of Windsor Park in the background, U class locos, No 200 *Lough Melvin* of the 1915 batch and an unidentified 1948 engine stand over the pits outside the shed.** Ian Allan Library.

Below: **After the UTA takeover, ex-NCC engines displaced by dieselisation began to operate on the former GNR lines. A NCC W class 2-6-0 is glimpsed between two GNR U class 4-4-0s, No 202 *Louth* now** UTA No 67 and No 200 *Lough Melvin* now No 65. Also in the picture is the other *Lough Melvin*, the ex-SLNCR 0-6-4 tank acquired by the UTA following that line's closure in 1957. John Dewing.

ADELAIDE STATION

Top left: **A classic view of the 'Enterprise Express' picking up speed as it leaves the city and approaches Adelaide station. The lines leading to the shed are to the left of the train, which on 13th May 1948, is headed by the now preserved V class 4-4-0 No 85** *Merlin.* John Dewing.

Centre left: **S class No 170** *Errigal* **passes through Adelaide station with a train from Dublin on 26th May 1953. This view gives some idea of the huge expanse of land which the railway owned around here. The shed was built on part of a tract of marshy land known as the Bog Meadows, a title which tells its own story. Now covered with industrial and retail estates, only a few sidings remain in railway use on the site.** Neil Sprinks.

Bottom left: **Adelaide station on 13th May 1950, with 4-4-2 tank No 143 calling on an evening service to Antrim. The several footbridges in the vicinity provided good vantage points for photographers.** H C Casserley.

Pictures on the opposite page:

Top: **As we leave Belfast and head down the Lagan Valley, we see a four car diesel unit, including a buffet car, headed by Railcar No 618, speeding through Lambeg in August 1952. When the line opened in 1839 the only stopping place between Belfast and Lisburn was at Dunmurry. In time a further six stations or halts were added to cater for the growing commuter traffic into the city.** Ian Allan Library.

Bottom: **A short distance beyond Lambeg, in the Lisburn direction, a halt was opened at Hilden in 1907. Here, on 18th May 1960, U class No 196** *Lough Gill,* **renumbered 64 by the UTA, heads a service from Great Victoria Street to Antrim. I have always thought that the formation down the Lagan Valley to Lisburn looks rather wider than that on the rest of the system. Perhaps this is fanciful or it may be a legacy from the original Ulster Railway line, built to a gauge of 6ft 2in.** John Dewing.

LISBURN

Top left: **Lisburn was, and still is, a busy place though the number of destinations which can be reached from its three platforms is now much reduced. On 10th June 1949, P class No 104, one of the members of this class with the smaller 5ft 6in wheels, pauses at the outer face of Lisburn's island platform with the 2.12pm Banbridge to Great Victoria Street service.**

Centre left: **Another service off this long-closed line features in our second view of Lisburn station. One of the versatile UG 0-6-0s, No 78, built at Dundalk in 1937, pauses at the down main line platform with the 1.45pm Newcastle to Belfast train on the same day. On the GNR, as was the case with the other railways serving Dublin, the up line led to that city.** Both, SLS collection.

Below: **In February 1964, not long before the UTA terminated goods services on the railway system in Northern Ireland, SG3 No 35 (formerly GNR No 49) pounds along between Knockmore Junction and Lisburn with the heavy 2.45pm goods from Portadown to the Grosvenor Road goods yard in Belfast.** Derek Young.

THE ANTRIM BRANCH

Right: **A mile beyond Lisburn was situated Knockmore Junction where the lines to Banbridge and Antrim branched off the main line. Knockmore Junction cabin always struck me as being far too small to be able to control such an important location, but manned by a dynasty of signalmen named Mulholland it managed the job. The signalman is on his platform waiting to take the single line staff off the fireman of SG class 0-6-0 No 179, which brings its goods train off the Antrim branch and onto the main line.**

Centre right: **The only engineering feature of note on the line was the viaduct at Crumlin. UG class No 145 brings a goods train over the viaduct and is about to enter Crumlin station.** Both, Desmond Coakham.

Below: **The 18 mile long GNR branch terminated in the NCC station at Antrim whose citizens had the choice of two ways of getting to Belfast, though the NCC line was much shorter and quicker. The single road GNR engine shed is seen to the left of T2 class 4-4-2T No 62 at the head of the 1.55pm service to Great Victoria Street, on 10th June 1949. To the right of the picture, passing the distinctive somersault signal, is ex-NCC now UTA, A1 class 4-4-0 No 69 *Slieve Bane*, at the head of a short freight on the NCC up line heading for Belfast.** SLS collection.

Above: **Following our brief excursion up the Antrim branch, we return to Knockmore Junction to explore the second line which branched off from the main line here: that to Banbridge and Newcastle. This line is seen here striking** off to the left of the three coach railcar set, on a Dublin to Belfast working on 2nd August 1954. Ian Allan Library.

Opposite page top left: **In this close-up view of the bracket signal which controlled the junction, the arms to the left and right are those for the Banbridge and Antrim lines respectively. Below the main line home signal in the centre is the distant reading to an outer home signal installed in the 1950s.** Desmond Coakham.

THE BANBRIDGE LINE

Opposite page bottom: **The line to Banbridge opened in 1863 and was extended to Ballyroney in 1880 and Castlewellan in 1906. Here it made an end-on junction with a BCDR line, opened the same year, coming north from Newcastle. The GNR had running powers over this line to allow its trains to reach Newcastle. After leaving Knockmore Junction, trains passed Newforge siding which served a rendering factory and remained open until 1965, and Newport Halt opened in 1942. The line then reached Hillsborough. The station had a single platform but trains could cross at a passing loop which was just beyond the station. UG No 80 pauses at the platform; the points leading to the loop are directly in front of the loco.** This picture and the three to the right on this page; Drew Donaldson, courtesy W T Scott.

Above right: **A long cattle train hauled by QG class 0-6-0 No 153 enters the loop at Hillsborough in the summer of 1955.**

Centre right: **The next stopping place after Hillsborough was Ballygowan Halt opened in 1929. U class 4-4-0 No 197 _Lough Neagh_ calls there with a single coach train in September 1952.**

Bottom right: **Some 8½ miles from Knockmore Junction was Dromore. The fine seven arch viaduct over the River Lagan still exists here. SG3 class 0-6-0 No 8 brings a short goods from Banbridge into the station in 1954.**

BANBRIDGE STATION

Left: **Banbridge station was 15 miles from Knockmore Junction. Just outside the station was the junction with the branch from Scarva, on the GNR's Belfast to Dublin line. The Scarva branch, built by the Banbridge Junction Railway, was actually the first line to serve the town, opening in 1859, four years before that of the Banbridge, Lisburn & Belfast Railway's route to Knockmore. On 25th April 1951, UG class 0-6-0 No 146 arrives at Banbridge with the 3.25pm service from Belfast.** John Edgington.

Above: **A busy scene at Banbridge station on 1st January 1955. On the left of the picture, UG No 145 shunts in the goods yard. Railcar A in the bay platform was working the Scarva branch that day. In the down platform, a set of AEC railcars are on a Belfast to Newcastle service. These are crossing a train for Belfast hauled by SG3 class 0-6-0 No 48.** Lance King.

Left: **UG No 146 is seen taking a short goods train out of Banbridge's goods yard which, as seen above, was located beside the passenger station. This locomotive, which theoretically was built for goods traffic, is equipped with both vacuum brake and steam heating pipes, confirmation that these were in reality mixed traffic engines, as much at home on passenger trains as on goods workings.** Bobby Brown collection.

THE SCARVA BRANCH

Right: **The line from Banbridge to Scarva was 6¾ miles in length. In the 1950s there was only one proper station open on the line, that at Laurencetown. However, the line was normally worked by a railcar and there were requests stops at virtually every level crossing on the branch. Railcar A, working the 12.55pm from Banbridge to Scarva on 28th June 1952, approaches one of these stopping places, Hazlebank level crossing.** Neil Sprinks.

Centre: **The ubiquitous railcar A pauses at Laurencetown, whose station nameboard had seen better days. This shows Railcar A in its later condition (compare this with the photo on page 21); the original radiator has been replaced and the space panelled over. The radiator is now on the roof.** Bobby Brown collection.

Below: **Many services on the branch carried on through Scarva to Goraghwood or down the branch from there to Newry and Warrenpoint. This view looking south shows the bay platform for the branch trains at Scarva. U class 4-4-0 No 200, is at the head of the single coach which will form the 5.10pm to Banbridge on 10th June 1949. This locomotive, one of the early members of the class dating from 1915, did not receive its name *Lough Melvin* until 1950. The line from Banbridge to Scarva was closed in May 1955 by the GNRB.** SLS collection.

ON TO NEWCASTLE

Above: **Back at Banbridge, we will resume our journey to Newcastle in the company of U class 4-4-0 No 197 which is at the head of the 4.55pm Great Victoria Street to Newcastle train on 10th June 1949. The five 1915-built U class engines were given names between 1949 and 1953. Nos 197 and 199 were the first to be so endowed. No 197's new nameplate (she was called *Lough Neagh*) and her lined blue livery are apparent in this view.** SLS collection.

Centre left: **The first station south of Banbridge was at Corbet. On 17th May 1955 another U class locomotive, No 196, now named *Lough Gill*, a 1915 machine but here paired with one of the later tenders, is seen at the single platform station.** Bobby Brown collection.

Bottom left: **This is one for those who enjoy railway quizzes, though it is something of a trick question I fear. Question, in what county was Leitrim station? Answer, County Down of course. The station was 14 miles from Banbridge. This view taken from a departing train on 14th April 1953 is looking back in the direction of Newcastle. Services along the line as far as Banbridge lasted until April 1956. The remainder of the route, from Banbridge through to Castlewellan and Newcastle, was closed in May 1955.**
H C Casserley.

Above: **At Castlewellan the trains of two companies could be seen side by side. The GNR extended its line from Ballyroney in March 1906 to coincide with the opening of the BCDR branch from Newcastle which made an end-on junction with the GNR line. On 10th June 1949, U class No 197, on the 4.55pm Great Victoria Street to Newcastle service, awaits the arrival of ex-BCDR, now UTA, 4-4-2T No 3 on the 5.40pm from Belfast Queen's Quay to Castlewellan, via Newcastle.**

Centre: **The GNR had running powers over the BCDR line into Newcastle. Citizens of and visitors to this attractive seaside town, where in the words of the ballad, 'the mountains of Mourne sweep down to the sea', had the choice of two services to Belfast. In this May 1948 view, BCDR 4-4-2 T No 21 is at the head of the 4.28pm train to Belfast Queen's Quay. The GNR stock which will form the 5.00pm to Great Victoria Street is at the other platform. On 1st October 1948, the BCDR was taken over by the UTA who closed the entire system, with the exception of the Bangor branch, in 1950. Newcastle retained a service to Belfast via Castlewellan until 2nd May 1955 when the line from Newcastle to Banbridge also succumbed.**

Bottom: **With BCDR signals in the background, GNR 0-6-0 No 40, a locomotive built originally for the D&BJR in 1872, rests between duties at Newcastle in the summer of 1936, the year before its withdrawal.** All photos, SLS collection.

LURGAN

Above: **Following our rambles in County Down, it is back to the main line to continue our journey on towards Dublin.**

On 1st February 1964, the former GNR S class 4-4-0 No 170 *Errigal*, is seen approaching Lurgan with the 1.05pm local service from Belfast to Portadown. This was one of several GNR locomotives bought from CIE in 1963 by the UTA to cover a temporary shortage of motive power.

Below: **SG2 No 38, the former GNR No 16, passes through Lurgan station with the 10.32am goods train from the Grosvenor Road goods depot in Belfast to Portadown in February 1964.** Both, Ian Allan Library.

PORTADOWN STATION

Left: **Portadown was an important station in its own right and a major junction. It will be the starting point for two other chapters in this book when we explore the Derry Road and follow the erstwhile Ulster Railway main line to Armagh and Clones. Here a stopping service from Belfast headed by 4-4-2 T No 116 arrives at the station on 26th June 1952.** Neil Sprinks.

Above: **A classic view of Portadown as I remember it in UTA days when ex-GNR and NCC locomotives shared duties on the former GNR lines. On 13th July 1963, VS class, UTA No 58 (GNR No 208)** *Lagan* **comes off a Derry train on which it will be replaced by S class No 170** *Errigal*, **on the right of the picture, whilst WT class 2-6-4 No 53 is running round the stock it has recently brought in on a local service from Belfast.**

Left: **On 5th July 1961, UG class 0-6-0 No 49 (GNR No 149), built by Beyer Peacock in 1948, the last of the long line of engines of this wheel arrangement delivered to the Great Northern, leaves Portadown with the 6.24pm train to Warrenpoint.** Both, Des Fitzgerald

PORTADOWN JUNCTION

Above: **This view of Portadown Junction was taken from the signal cabin which controlled it. A three coach AEC railcar set comes round the sharp curve off the Dublin line. The tracks to its right lead to** Armagh; those diverging to the extreme right of the picture are those of the Derry Road. Portadown shed's impressive roundhouse, one of only two such structures on the GNR (the other was at Clones) occupies the space between the Dublin and Armagh lines. An SG3 sits in the headshunt outside the engine shed. Today all that remains is the sharply curved line to Dublin. The 'Enterprise' still has to slowly and noisily grind its way round this curve. Ian Allan Library.

Below: **In this closer view of the roundhouse, S class 4-4-0 No 173 Galtee More simmers on the turntable at Portadown shed in June 1955.** SLS collection.

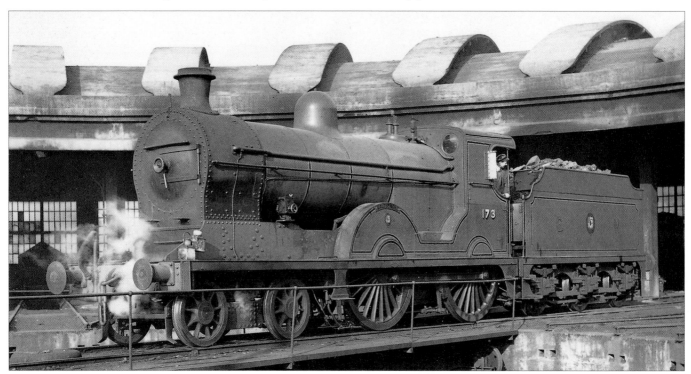

HEADING SOUTH

Top right: **After leaving Portadown the main line has easy gradients for the first 15 or so miles to beyond Poyntzpass. It passes over a tract of marshy ground running parallel with the disused Newry Canal for part of the way. The first station south of the junction was at Tanderagee. On 13th July 1962 U class No 68 (GNR No 205)** *Down* **brings a train of empty stock from Portadown, bound for Scarva, through this station.** Des Fitzgerald.

Centre right: **Just after Poyntzpass station, the line curves sharply and soon begins the long climb through Goraghwood to its summit at milepost 65½. Here, a four car railcar set leans on the curve as it heads south on a Belfast to Dublin working.** Ian Allan Library.

Bottom: **On Saturday 28th June 1952, the 12.00 Belfast to Dublin express was formed of 11 coaches including a restaurant car. The weight of the train meant that a pilot locomotive was required for the climb up to Bessbrook. QL class 4-4-0 No 24, built in 1910, double-heads VS class No 208** *Lagan*. **The train is seen leaving Poyntzpass. The signal cabin here was the last GNR box to survive in Northern Ireland. The cabin and its GNR semaphore signals remained in service until the mid 1990s.** Neil Sprinks.

GORAGHWOOD

Above: **The up 'Enterprise' was well into the long climb, with stretches as steep as 1 in 100, when it reached Goraghwood. Most trains had to stop here for examination by H M Customs. The revolutionary, for the time, feature of the 'Enterprise Express', introduced in August 1947, was that customs examinations took place at either terminus and the train could thus run non-stop between Belfast and Dublin. On 9th June 1954, VS class No 208 *Lagan* brings this service through Goraghwood. The quarry in the background was used to supply ballast to the company.**

Centre left: **Goraghwood was the junction for the erstwhile Newry & Armagh line, the northern part of which, from here to Armagh, lost its passenger services in 1933. The remaining part of this route and its continuation to Warrenpoint survived until 1965. In August 1959 the former GNR railcar D, renumbered 103 by the UTA, pauses at Goraghwood's up platform, with a service from Warrenpoint to Portadown. Both, Ian Allan Library.**

Bottom left: **With the main line on the embankment behind it, 4-4-2T No 186 leaves Goraghwood with the 11.15am train to Warrenpoint on 4th June 1954.** Neil Sprinks.

NEWRY

Top right: **There was a stiff climb for trains leaving Newry, which was virtually at sea level, up to the junction. The branch was particularly busy in summer with visitors travelling to enjoy the delights of the seaside at Warrenpoint. On Sunday 21st June 1964 UG No 49 (GNR No 149) is working hard up the bank to Goraghwood with the 4.10pm from Warrenpoint.**

Centre right: **Newry had two GNR stations and five level crossings. The more important of the two stations was that at Edward Street, seen in these views. On 4th July 1961 UTA No 65 (GNR No 200) *Lough Melvin* leaves the station with the 5.30pm train to Warrenpoint.** Both, Des Fitzgerald.

Below: **This general view of Newry Edward Street was taken in August 1937. Looking towards Warrenpoint, the GNR engine shed is seen on the left of the picture. Edward Street was, until the line closed in 1952, the terminus of trains from Greenore on that part of the former Dundalk, Newry & Greenore Railway, a little piece of the English London & North Western Railway on the wrong side of the Irish Sea. The working of this line had been entrusted to the GNR since 1933.** Ian Allan Library.

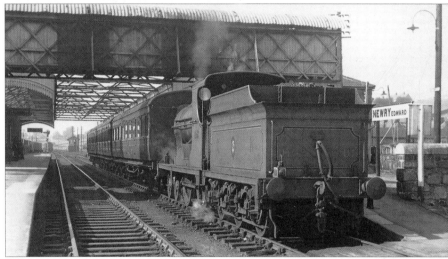

Above: **This is Newry's other GNR station, Dublin Bridge, located less than a mile from Edward Street in the direction of Warrenpoint. I have been careful to use the term GNR to describe the two stations illustrated, as up to 1952, the town had a third station, Bridge Street, which was on the DN&G line again less than a mile from Edward Street. UG No 48, the former GNR No 146, pauses at Dublin Bridge station with a train for Warrenpoint in July 1964. One of the five level crossings, Dublin Bridge Station Gates, is seen behind the train.** Ian Allan Library.

Centre left: **Newry was also a port, at the end of the navigable river which empties into Carlingford Lough. A line ran to Albert Basin, on the Newry Canal, from King Street Junction, between Edward Street and Dublin Bridge. On 31st March 1964, the coaster *Oak*, registered in Newry, is seen discharging coal into railway wagons at Albert Basin.** John Langford.

Bottom left: **Newry, with its canal and rivers, three stations and five level crossings, must have been a fascinating place in its heyday. Trains bound for Warrenpoint, shortly after leaving Dublin Bridge station, had to cross the Clanrye River on this bridge. Here a train from Warrenpoint on Easter Tuesday, 16th April 1963, hauled by UTA No 67 (GNR No 202) *Louth*, trundles over the bridge.** Des Fitzgerald.

WARRENPOINT

Top right: **Like all the other railway-served seaside towns around the shores of these islands, Warrenpoint attracted its fair share of day trippers on summer Sundays. This led to trains being strengthened to cope with the extra passengers wanting to take the sea air. Viewed from the top of Narrow Water Castle on the shore of Carlingford Lough, S class No 63 (GNR No 192) *Slievenamon* hauls the seven coach 4.10pm Warrenpoint to Goraghwood service, on Sunday 9th August 1964.** Noel Machell/Ian Allan Library.

Centre right: **1964 was the last summer for the line which the UTA closed in January 1965. On Sunday 30th August of that year, UG No 48 (GNR No 146) is seen near Narrow Water with the same 4.10pm service to Goraghwood, this time consisting of six bogies.** Derek Young.

Below: **Away from busy Sundays, two or three coaches were usually sufficient for the traffic on offer. Seen at Warrenpoint on 4th July 1961, U class No 65 (GNR No 200) *Lough Melvin* is at the head of a more typical formation. The branch had a good service of about eight or nine trains each way in the early 1950s. Most of these ran through to Portadown or even Belfast and the articulated railcars, such as E and F, were regular performers on its services.** Des Fitzgerald.

Top left: **Warrenpoint station, like so many on the GNR, was built with the attractive and distinctive yellow glazed bricks favoured by the first civil engineer of the newly amalgamated company, William Mills. Stations of broadly similar design, alongside which were houses of a standard design for the station master, were to be seen all over Great Northern territory. On 28th April 1956, railcar F has just arrived with the 3.52pm from Goraghwood. The next service to the junction, the 4.22pm departure, will be worked by 4-4-2T No 116.** John Edgington.

Centre left: **Warrenpoint, like Newry, was a port and this brought a lot of goods traffic to the branch. SG2 class 0-6-0 No 40 (GNR No 18) is shunting goods wagons at the station in August 1964.** Ian Allan Library.

Below: **The 12th of July was always a busy day for the railways of Ulster. Those marching in Orange demonstrations around the province needed transport to take them to the venues for their parades. Many of those not involved in the demonstrations would head for the seaside. To this day, the 12th Fortnight is still the peak holiday season in the province, even if the preferred destination these days is more likely to be Benidorm rather than Bundoran. A typical 12th of July brought a lot of extra traffic to Warrenpoint as may be seen from this view taken on the line's final 12th, that in 1964. UG No 48 (GNR No 146) is flanked by two S class locomotives. On its left is No 60 (GNR No 172) Slieve Donard, and on its right, No 171 Slieve Gullion.**
W G Sumner/Ian Allan Library.

CRAIGMORE

Top: **Back on the main line about two miles south of Goraghwood is located one of the great civil engineering masterpieces of the Irish railway system, the 18 arch Craigmore viaduct. VS class 4-4-0 No 58** (GNR No 208) *Lagan* **has still over four miles to climb to reach the summit on 4th July 1961 with the 8.15am Belfast to Dublin train.** Des Fitzgerald.

Above: **Immediately south of the viaduct was Bessbrook station. Closed in 1942, a new station was opened here in 1984 called Newry. Though the line through** Newry closed in 1965, the growing town, indeed now the city of Newry, has stretched up the hill towards the main line in the intervening years. This was history repeating itself as the original D&BJR station, opened here in 1855, was also called Newry. *Lagan* **is again the loco on this southbound working coming off the viaduct in July 1963.** Ian Allan Library.

Above: **This is one of the classic images of the Great Northern. On 20th May 1949, when the locomotive was less than a year old and with the 'Enterprise Express' only in its third year of operation, VS class No 208 *Lagan* was recorded working hard near Adavoyle by one of our finest railway photographers, John Dewing.**

Below: **Once they were over the summit at milepost 65½ southbound trains had favourable gradients down to Dundalk. However, those heading north out of the town faced 11 miles of adverse gradients, with some stretches as steep as 1 in 100, before they reached the summit. This long drag past the closed stations and lonely signal cabins at Mount Pleasant and Adavoyle, was what lay in store for this heavy northbound express, seen passing**

Dundalk North cabin at the start of its climb on 14th April 1948. The train engine, V class 4-4-0 No 83 *Eagle*, still in original condition with its round-topped firebox, is piloted by the then brand new U class 4-4-0, No 204 *Antrim*. The man who recorded this scene is another of the great railway photographers of the last century, the late Henry Casserley.

DUNDALK

Above: **Dundalk was a major railway centre. The site of the GNR's works, it was also the junction for the former Irish North Western lines and the DN&G route to Greenore (see pages 92 and 93). The station consisted of a broad island platform which was connected to the** main building by a footbridge. **There was a bay platform at the Dublin end of the station and through lines and sidings flanked the up and down main lines which were served by the island platform. Stopping cross border trains were examined by the Irish Customs here. On 14th April 1948, S class 4-4-0 No 192** Slievenamon **is seen at the up platform on such a working.** H C Casserley.

Below: **V class compound 4-4-0 No 83** Eagle **leaves Dundalk with an express for Dublin on 12th June 1954. This view shows the main station building to the right of the picture and the footbridge which connected it to the island platform. The bay platform is to the left of the locomotive.** C H A Townley.

Opposite page top: **Immediately after leaving the station came the junction for Irish North, then Dundalk Square Crossing (see page 93), part of which is in the foreground in this picture. The main line then passed the GNR works. The siding beside the down line which ended at the crossing was often used to store ex-works locomotives. Here V class No 84 *Falcon* on a Belfast train passes sister locomotive No 85 *Merlin*, which has just come out of the works. This undated view may have been taken in 1950 when No 85 was rebuilt with a square-topped Belpaire**

boiler. She was the last of the compounds to receive this, No 84 obtained hers in 1947. John Edgington collection.

Opposite page bottom: **In immaculate condition, probably just ex-works, U class No 204 *Antrim* is seen at Dundalk running shed on 26th April 1951.** John Edgington.

Above: **Crane tank, No 31, is shunting at the works in May 1950. The building to the left is the Carriage Shop.** H C Casserley.

Bottom right: **When the whole S class was completely renewed in 1938/39 at the works, they also received the blue livery and had their nameplates restored. No 173 *Galtee More* gleams in the Paint Shop in May 1938, her overhaul nearly complete.** Ian Allan Library.

Bottom left: **On the turntable at the works in the CIE era, in front of the General Stores building, is Q class 4-4-0 No 132. Sheerlegs used for lifting locomotives to remove their wheels can just be seen to the left of the picture.** Ian Allan Library.

DROMIN JUNCTION

Above: **After passing through the wayside station of Castlebellingham, 10 miles south of Dundalk came Dromin Junction, where the branch to Ardee, which opened in 1896, met the main line. Though the** branch lost its passenger service in 1934, goods services continued into the 1970s and several GNR bus routes also served the town. On 23rd May 1958, the 'Enterprise Express' formed of the new BUT railcars, speeds through Dromin Junction as NQG class 0-6-0 No 112 waits in the bay platform with the Ardee goods. John Edgington.

Below: **The branch to Ardee was five miles long and had no intermediate stations. Here an unidentified 0-6-0 shunts at its terminus. The long-abandoned passenger station is behind the train. The tall structures in the middle of the picture are the silos belonging to the Ardee Grain Company.** Ian Allan Library.

DROGHEDA

Top right: **The GNR main line continued south through Dunleer climbing steadily to a summit at Kellystown Signal Box. From there the gradient was in favour of southbound trains as far as Drogheda. At Newfoundwell, just north of the town, the site of the original D&BJR station before the Boyne viaduct was built, a branch to a cement factory came in on the up side. NQG class 0-6-0 No 38 waits to leave the branch at its junction with the main line on 19th June 1958.**

Centre right: **Earlier in the day the same locomotive is seen shunting at the factory. The railway viaduct over the Boyne may just be glimpsed in the background above the wagons on the left.** Both, A E Bennett.

Below: **The famous viaduct itself is seen here, with an S class locomotive bringing what is probably the 'Bundoran Express' into Drogheda station. When the viaduct opened for traffic in April 1855, after many vicissitudes, the through route between Belfast and Dublin was at last completed. As built, it carried double track. However, by the end of the nineteenth century it was beginning to show signs of age and strict weight limits were imposed on it. Eventually only one train at a time was allowed on the viaduct. The structure was finally renewed between 1930 and 1932 allowing heavier locomotives such as the new V class compounds and the SG3 goods engines to use it.** Ian Allan Library.

THE OLDCASTLE BRANCH

Left: **Drogheda station is located on a sharp curve at the end of the Boyne viaduct. This was the junction for the branch to Navan and Oldcastle. On 23rd April 1956, railcar A is seen at the down main line platform before working the 3.40pm service to Oldcastle. The branch joined the main line at the south end of the station. Trains had to reverse to reach the platforms. In this view the radiators on the roof of Railcar A, referred to earlier (see page 41) can be seen more clearly.** Ian Allan Library.

Above: **Beauparc was 11 miles from Drogheda. On 7th May 1955, Railcar A, which was forming the 10.10am Navan to Drogheda service, crosses SG class No 178 which was hauling the 9.55am Drogheda to Oldcastle train.**

Left: **The main town served by the branch was Navan. The line approached the town's station from the Drogheda direction on another fine viaduct over the River Boyne. Here, a special train leaves Navan hauled by a Q class 4-4-0.** Both, Ian Allan Library.

Top right: **The first station at Navan had been on the other side of the Boyne. The GNR station, another of the company's yellow brick structures, had only one platform, though there was a passing loop. Passenger services between Drogheda and Oldcastle ended in April 1958, though the line is still open for goods traffic from the nearby Tara Mines. Here, SG2 class 0-6-0 No 17 is seen at the station on a goods train.** Ian Allan Library.

Centre right: **Just west of the GNR station was Navan Junction, where the former MGWR line from Clonsilla met the GNR line. The Midland line which continued on to Kingscourt in County Cavan was seen by the GNR as a sign of that company's aggressive intention to muscle in on its territory. In this view, a former MGWR 0-6-0 is seen at the Midland side of the junction station; the GNR line is to the left of the signal box.** Ian Allan Library.

Below: **Oldcastle was nearly 40 miles from Drogheda. Trains took around an hour and a half for the journey. Typical of the service was that shown in the 1952 Summer timetable. There were only two through trains in each direction, one in the morning and one in the afternoon and no Sunday service, though there were three additional short return workings from Drogheda to Navan. Oldcastle was a typical branch line terminus. On 2nd May 1938, PPs class 4-4-0 No 50 was the engine on duty. The single road engine shed is to the right and the station, with its train shed, is in the distance.** SLS collection.

Top left: **A new station was opened six miles south of Drogheda in 1948. This was Mosney, built to serve the adjacent Butlin's Holiday Camp. It had a signal box and its one platform was on a loop off the down line. It was not advertised in the timetables until 1958, but some local services terminated there despite this. A sea mist is rolling in on 23rd April 1956 as 4-4-2T No 67 prepares to return to Amiens Street.** John Edgington.

Centre left: **Continuing coal shortages after the Second World War encouraged the GNR to experiment with oil firing. Four 4-4-2Ts, Nos 1, 2, 115 and 116, were converted to burn oil in 1946. They were all converted back to coal firing in 1948. No 2, seen here leaving Balbriggan with a local service to Amiens Street on 16th May 1948, was still oil fired at this time. It is producing plenty of black smoke though this might be expected whatever fuel was being used, as it has a heavy eight bogie train to cope with. The oil tank can just be seen rising above the bunker behind the driving cab.** John Dewing.

Below: **South from Drogheda, the line is never far from the coast. Approaching Malahide, it crosses an inlet of the sea on a long low viaduct. On 27th September 1959, No 58 (GNR No 208) *Lagan* is seen on Malahide viaduct with a special from Belfast to Dublin.** J C Natzio.

THE HOWTH BRANCH

Top right: **The short 3½ mile long branch from Howth Junction to Howth was opened in 1846 by the Dublin & Drogheda Railway. It had always carried a healthy passenger traffic consisting of both commuters and day trippers. Up to 1973, when Bayside station was opened by CIE, there had been only one station on the line, at Sutton. For many years after the final abandonment of the Dublin tramway system in 1949, a couple of trams were dumped in a field near Sutton station. Here, SG3 class 0-6-0 No 48, paired with a modern tender, approaches Sutton on 15th June 1958.** A E Bennett.

Centre right: **On 27th May 1958, 4-4-2T No 62, an example of a class often seen on Howth trains, arrives at Sutton and Baldoyle, to give the station its full name, with the 5.15pm train from Amiens Street to Howth.** John Edgington.

Below: **Howth Junction, 4¾ miles from Amiens Street, was distinguished by tall semaphores and and a fine display of foliage in the space between the up main line and down branch platforms. On 18th May 1959, Q class 4-4-0 No 131 speeds through the station with a Belfast to Dublin express. This area is heavily built up and the now electrified Howth branch is busier than ever.** John Dewing.

APPROACHING DUBLIN

Left: **The GNR always provided a decent service of local trains from Amiens Street to Howth and out as far as Drogheda on the main line. Since the 1950s, this part of Dublin has seen a huge amount of housing development. A three coach railcar train calls at one of these suburban stations, Raheny, on 31st March 1954. The prospect then was largely rural; this is certainly not the case today.**

Below: **Trains faced a climb out of Amiens Street as far as Raheny. Tackling the bank on 29th May 1955, with a Belfast train, is VS class 4-4-0 No 206 *Liffey*.** Both, Neil Sprinks.

Left: **On 13th August 1952, a Howth train headed by T2 class No 144, is seen on the bridge over the Howth Road where the original Clontarf station was located. Leaving Dublin, the line crossed the River Tolka and ran along the embankment at Fairview which had reclaimed from the sea the tract of land which is now Fairview Park. For many years this was used as a rubbish tip for the city. Landfill was brought to the site at night on wagons hauled by electric locomotives on the city's tramways. In the 1950s, the GNR built a railcar maintenance depot here, now expanded and used by the DART electric units.** John Dewing.

AMIENS STREET

Above: **On the evening of 8th December 1954, heavy rain in the Dublin area turned the Tolka River into a raging torrent which swept away the bridge carrying the railway. Alternative arrangements were made for the traffic and a temporary bridge was erected with commendable speed. On 30th December No 84 *Falcon* brings a test train of loaded cement wagons gingerly on to the temporary bridge watched by workmen and bystanders.**

Centre right: **In the late 1940s S class 4-4-0 No 173 *Galtee More* leaves the GNR terminus in Dublin, Amiens Street station, with an express for Belfast which includes dining cars.** Both, Ian Allan Library.

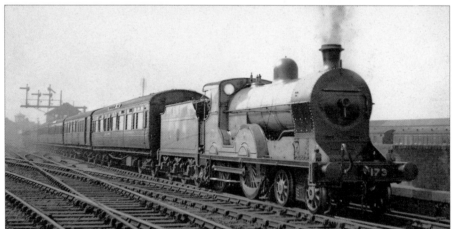

Bottom right: **Railcars No 619, with 618 at the other end of the two trailers, arrive at Amiens Street on a local service. Unless separated by a mechanical failure, the AEC railcars usually operated in numerically sequential pairs! The track in the foreground is that of the Howth bay; the lines to the left of the signal box are those leading to the loop line across the River Liffey and on to Westland Row station.** F W Shuttleworth.

Above: **Amiens Street was and is both a terminus and a through station. This short platform outside the protection of the station's overall roof was often the starting point for trains to Howth. Railcar F was on such a duty when seen at the station. This view shows how the two passenger saloons were articulated from the engine unit in the centre of the set.** Ian Allan Library.

Centre left: **From October 1950 until 1953, the morning working of the 'Enterprise Express' was extended to run through to Cork. The GNR and CIE both provided sets of coaches for this service and locomotives were exchanged at Amiens Street. The train from Belfast would run into one of the through platforms and a CIE locomotive would come onto the other end of the set to take the train round the city via Glasnevin Junction and the tunnel under the Phoenix Park, to join the Cork main line at Islandbridge Junction just outside Kingsbridge station. Here CIE B2a class 4-6-0 No 406 prepares to leave Amiens Street for Cork. In 1952 the train left Belfast at 10.30am, arrived at Amiens Street at 12.45pm, where 45 minutes were allowed for engine changing and other station duties. With a stop at Limerick Junction, it arrived in Cork at 5.15pm. In the other direction, the train left Cork at 1.15pm, arriving in Belfast at 7.45pm that evening.** Ian Allan Library.

Bottom left: **With a railcar in the Howth bay, V class compound No 85 *Merlin*, sanders in use to keep her 6ft 7in driving wheels from slipping on this damp day, accelerates out of Amiens Street with the 9.00am train to Belfast on 20th March 1954.** Neil Sprinks.

THE DERRY ROAD

The Great Northern route from Belfast to Derry was about five miles longer than the other line between these two northern cities, that from Belfast York Road to Waterside station in Londonderry, on the opposite bank of the River Foyle to the GNR's Foyle Road terminus. What became the GNR line was built in two parts. The section from Derry to Omagh was opened in stages between 1847 and 1852 by the Londonderry & Enniskillen Railway. The other part of the route, from Portadown Junction to Dungannon, was opened in 1858 and from there to Omagh in 1862, by the Portadown, Dungannon & Omagh Railway, a company heavily backed by the Ulster Railway.

The section from Portadown to Dungannon was relatively flat. Apart from a viaduct over the River Blackwater at Vernersbridge, the only engineering feature of note was a tunnel of about 800 yards in length, just south of Dungannon station, built at the insistence of the local landowner, Lord Northland, who did not want the view across his estate spoiled by the passage of trains. Beyond Dungannon, the railway had to cross the foothills of the Sperrin Mountains. The summit of this eight mile climb was between Pomeroy and Carrickmore. The line was as steep as 1 in 70 and 1 in 80 in short stretches on either side of the summit which at 561 feet above sea level was the highest point on the GNR, though the short-lived and long-closed Castleblayney to Keady line had once scaled a greater height than this.

Leaving the bleak Sperrin uplands behind, the nature of the line changed again north of Omagh as it followed the valleys of the Strule and Mourne rivers to reach Strabane, crossing these rivers seven times on this wonderfully picturesque stretch of railway. The final 15 miles into Derry followed the County Donegal bank of the River Foyle and were virtually level.

The 1960s were a whacky and surreal decade in many ways. One mantra of the transport planners of the era was that there should be only one railway route between two places. In the south this logic had seen off the Harcourt Street line from Dublin to Bray in 1958, another line, like the Derry Road, which should never have closed, but unlike our line, one which is being revived. Add to this the UTA's antipathy to railways, the Stormont government's passion for roads and a much whispered but never proven conspiracy on the part of those in high places to isolate the west of the province and focus investment east of the River Bann, and the poor old Derry Road never had a chance. Its closure in February 1965 left that huge gap which today blemishes the railway map of Ireland. If you head due south from Derry today, you will not encounter a railway line with a passenger service until you reach Mullingar!

Top right: **The Derry Road left the main line to Dublin at Portadown Junction. In August 1959 U class No 67 (GNR No 202)** *Louth* **rounds the curve away from the Dublin line. Portadown Junction signal cabin is seen to the left of the picture.** Ian Allan Library.

Bottom right: **The first part of the route ran along easy gradients not far from the southern shore of Lough Neagh. This was an area of poor land and peat bogs, some of which had their own narrow gauge railway systems. The first station, about 6¾ miles from Portadown Junction, was at Annaghmore. The whole of what was to become the Derry Road was originally single track throughout. Growing traffic levels at the end of the nineteenth century led to the line from Portadown Junction to Trew & Moy being doubled between 1899 and 1902. The line remained single track from there through the tunnel into Dungannon, but the three mile section to Donaghmore was also doubled by 1906. This stretch was singled by the GNR in 1936, the UTA singling the longer double track section from Portadown to Trew & Moy in 1959. In UTA days UG No 47 (GNR No 82), the last new locomotive built at Dundalk works, pauses at Annaghmore with a local service between Portadown and Dungannon.** SLS collection.

DUNGANNON

Top left: **This is the west end of the unnecessary 814 yard long Dungannon tunnel, built at the insistence of the local big wig, Lord Northland, which so terrified me as a child.** Des Fitzgerald.

Top right: **Passenger trains on the Derry Road in GNR days were dominated by medium sized 4-4-0s such as the S and Q classes. The V and VS classes were too** heavy for use on the route. Here S class No 174 *Carrantuohill* leaves Dungannon station with a train for Belfast on 25th May 1952. Neil Sprinks.

Above: **The UTA dieselised passenger services on the former LMS/NCC lines to Larne and Londonderry using the versatile multiple purpose diesel railcars, which were introduced from 1957 onwards. However, the LMS had bequeathed to the UTA the most modern steam fleet in Ireland made up of the 17 WT class 2-6-4 tanks, built between 1946 and 1950 and the 15 W class Moguls dating from the** 1930s. With little work for these locomotives on their own lines, many were transferred by the UTA to Adelaide shed to work on the former GNR lines. The WTs were deemed too heavy for use on the Derry Road but the W class 2-6-0s were often used on both goods and passenger workings in the 1960s. Here No 99 *King George VI* is seen approaching Dungannon on 8th August 1964 with a goods train from Portadown. Jack Patience.

Top right: Dungannon station had three platforms. The outer face of the island platform was used by trains for the Cookstown branch which diverged half a mile north of the station. In this undated view, Q class 4-4-0 No 132, a type which were regular performers on the route for many decades, is about to depart with a train for Derry while an unidentified 0-6-0 is on the other side of the island platform with the connecting service to Cookstown. Ian Allan Library.

Centre right: In addition to the through trains from Belfast to Derry, local trains served various parts of the line. There were occasional services between Strabane and Derry, from Omagh to both Strabane and Dungannon, and from Dungannon to Portadown. Here SG No 44 (GNR No 176) is about to depart from Dungannon with the 4.40pm local service to Portadown on 30th June 1962. Des Fitzgerald.

Below: The 14½ mile long line from Dungannon to Cookstown was opened in 1879. It served the town of Coalisland, one of the few areas in Ireland where workable coal deposits were to be found. The branch had a reasonable service of six or seven trains in each direction until the passenger service was taken off in January 1956. On 26th June 1952, T2 class 4-4-2T No 69 is seen with the branch set at Dungannon station. Neil Sprinks.

THE COOKSTOWN BRANCH

Left: **Coalisland station was 5½ miles from Dungannon. The town was a veritable hive of industry. There was a siding nearby serving Annagher Colliery and further sidings were provided for the local brickworks and a sand quarry. The line from here to Cookstown closed completely in 1959, but the Coalisland to Dungannon section remained open for freight until January 1965.** Ian Allan Library.

Above: **Cookstown had two stations which were adjacent to each other. The first line to reach the town was a long branch, from Cookstown Junction on the NCC main line, which opened in 1856. This panoramic view of the extensive railway facilities at Cookstown was taken on 6th May 1948. The GNR station is on the extreme left of the picture. P class 4-4-0 No 73 is at the head of the 1.55pm service to Dungannon. At the platform of the adjacent NCC station are the coaches for the 2.35pm train to Belfast York Road. Shunting at the NCC goods shed is U1 class 4-4-0 No 4A *Glenariff*. To its left is the NCC shed. Finally, the locomotive to the right of the picture is U2 class 4-4-0 No 75 *Antrim Castle*.** Ian Allan Library.

Bottom left: **The UTA withdrew passenger services to Cookstown in August 1950, though the line remained open for goods traffic until May 1955. By the time this photograph was taken on 26th June 1952, therefore, only the GNR passenger service survived. T2 class 4-4-2T No 69 is seen on a passenger train for Dungannon.** Neil Sprinks.

Top right: **Back on the main line, on 23rd June 1964 SG2 class 0-6-0 No 38 (GNR No 16) passes through the now closed Donaghmore station with a goods train from Portadown to Derry.** Des Fitzgerald.

Centre right: **A feature of many GNR lines was that trains stopped at level crossings along the route. These stopping places did not usually appear in the public timetables though the trains which made such stops were identified with a letter at the head of the column and a footnote at the bottom of the table. This lack of clarity about places where trains did stop has long been a headache for those researching the history of these lines. The practice of stopping at level crossings coincided with the introduction of railcars and railbuses in the 1930s but in many instances steam trains covering such turns were required to make the stops as well. On 26th October 1957, passengers use steps to gain access to the 12.55pm train from Omagh to Dungannon, hauled by Q class No 122, as it pauses at Reynold's Crossing between Pomeroy and Donaghmore.** Drew Donaldson, courtesy W T Scott.

Below: **Railcar A pauses at Pomeroy in the summer of 1957. From Donaghmore the line had been climbing steadily and would reach its summit of 561ft above sea level at milepost 26½ between here and Carrickmore. Whilst steam trains laboured up the bank in both directions, I recall that the railcars, by comparison, used to fly up the incline.** Ian Allan Library.

Above: **SG2 No 42 (GNR No 183) pounds up the bank with an Apprentice Boys of Derry special train on 10th August 1963.** John Smallwood.

Left: **Carrickmore station was some distance from the village it was named after. Its location probably contributed to its premature closure in 1959.** Ian Allan Library.

Bottom left: **The next station after Carrickmore was Sixmilecross, four miles further on. This station had only a single platform.** Ian Allan Library.

Bottom right: **My heart quickens as we approach God's country. Two miles beyond Sixmilecross was Beragh and then it was on towards Omagh. Another Apprentice Boys special passes with SG2 No 17 at its head over the Leap Bridge which brought the line over the River Strule near Omagh.** Des Fitzgerald.

OMAGH

Right: **Less than a mile south of Omagh station was the junction for the Market Yard branch. The fireman of a goods train about to head down the short branch has set the points at the ground frame. During a bitter railway strike in 1933, a passenger train was derailed on these points.**

Below: **It may not be as glamorous as the end of one of the platforms at Paddington or Euston, but this is where my interest in**

railways was born, the goods station at the Market Yard in Omagh. SG3 No 14 is shunting there on 12th August 1957. Both, A E Bennett.

Bottom: **Q class No 136 brings a train from Belfast into Omagh, passing the town's engine shed on the right. Today all traces of the line have been obliterated under a new road which exactly replicates, down to the position of its bridges, the route of the old railway. In suitable deference to what went before, the new route is called Great Northern Road.** Ian Allan Library.

Top left: **Omagh was an important junction up until 1957 when the lines to Enniskillen and beyond were closed. The physical junction was at the end of the station's platforms and was controlled by Omagh South cabin. On 10th May 1956 PP class 4-4-0 No 106 arrives at Omagh on the 9.25am service from Enniskillen.** SLS collection.

Centre left: **The elegant, if elderly, P and PP class 4-4-0s were commonly used on services between Omagh and Enniskillen. On 1st June 1954, another PP class locomotive, No 74, is seen at Omagh station before departure with the 6.15pm train to Enniskillen.** Neil Sprinks.

Bottom: **A busy scene at the north end of Omagh station on 14th June 1949. On the left of the picture, U class 4-4-0 No 205 *Down* is detaching wagons from the rear of the 12.15pm train from Derry to Belfast. In the centre, Q class 4-4-0 No 124 has the road and is ready to depart with the 11.15am train from Belfast to Derry. This mid morning service usually had a restaurant car in its formation. In the bay platform to the right of the express is No 73, a member of the P class with the larger 6ft 6in driving wheels. It will work the 1.55pm slow train to Derry which will follow the express.** SLS collection.

Above left: **Omagh, the county town of Tyrone, right up to the closure of the line dealt with a large amount of goods traffic. As well as the goods depot at the Market Yard, there was a goods yard at the station. Here grain is being discharged from railway wagons into a vehicle operated by the local firm of millers, Scotts, whose lorries were a familiar sight in County Tyrone.** Desmond Coakham.

Above right: **A locomotive was usually based in Omagh to deal with the traffic at the two goods depots and that generated by a Nestlé factory at Conneywarren north of the town. By the 1960s, the engine shed, seen on page 73, was roofless and** derelict, **so engines were often stabled in the goods yard at the station where SG3 No 35 (GNR No 41) is seen out of steam over the Easter weekend of 1964.** John Langford.

Above: **LQG class No 109 is shunting at the north end of Omagh station after arriving with a goods train from Enniskillen on 1st June 1954. At the end of the station's platforms, on the morning of Friday 24th November 1950, a terrible tragedy occurred which led to the death of five railway workers. The period between 10 and 10.30am was a busy one. A train from Enniskillen was due at 10.17. This had to be shunted out of the way to allow trains** to and from Belfast to cross at around 10.30am. That morning there was thick fog and visibility was down to 10 or 15 yards in places. A permanent way gang was at work in the station. The fog and the noise from an engine on the adjacent line must have muted the sound of the train from Derry which ploughed into them. Two men were killed instantly, the other three died later in hospital. Their funerals were the biggest Omagh had ever seen. This decent town was not to experience such grief again until August 1998 when it was the victim of an act of unimaginable wickedness, against which even the events of November 1950 paled. Neil Sprinks.

NORTH OF OMAGH

Top left: **The line from Omagh to Derry had been opened between 1847 and 1852 by the Londonderry & Enniskillen Railway. After passing the siding which served the Nestlé milk processing factory (in Omaghspeak always pronounced Nestills, the subtleties of French pronunciation and acute accents being rather beyond us) the line reached the location of the former Mountjoy station. This had a chequered career, being open for three periods, from 1852-59, 1870-78 and finally 1928-35. On 8th August 1964, SG2 No 40 (GNR No 18) passes the site of the station with the 12.45pm extra for Strabane.**

Centre left: **'The Strule is rich with its gems and fishes', is the opening line of an old poem which my father, a very keen angler, used to recite to me. The railway followed the valleys of the rivers Strule and Mourne most of the way from a mile or so beyond Mountjoy to Strabane. I never came across any of the freshwater oysters referred to in the poem, but plenty of trout and the occasional salmon found their way onto the dinner tables of the towns and villages through which the rivers ran. The railway crossed the river seven times on this most picturesque 15 mile stretch of track. Standing on the high ground on either side of the valley, one could watch the progress of a steam train for miles. Crossing Blackrock Bridge between Omagh and Newtownstewart is the special train seen in the previous picture.** Both, Des Fitzgerald.

Bottom left: **Newtownstewart is ten miles north of Omagh. The station was some distance from the centre of the small town. On 21st May 1960, a three coach AEC railcar set pauses with a Derry to Belfast service at the station. The first two vehicles are in the UTA's dark green livery, the last car retains its GNR blue and cream colour scheme. Like most Derry Road services, there is a van at the rear to carry parcels and sundries. The UTA renumbered the GNR railcars it acquired, as well as the steam locomotives. The leading railcar No 112, was GNR No 602, one of the first of these railcars to enter service in 1950. Newtownstewart was a charming little station. It has a typical standard GNR signal cabin of a type seen all over the system and the main building, on the down (towards Derry) platform, is constructed of the yellow brick so beloved by the company.** John Dewing.

Top right: **The next station beyond Newtownstewart was at Victoria Bridge. Until it closed in 1933, this had been the terminus of the Castlederg & Victoria Bridge Tramway, a seven mile long 3ft gauge roadside tramway which had opened in 1884 to provide a railway connection to the small town of Castlederg, on the borders of the counties of Tyrone and Donegal. Here U class 4-4-0 No 67 (GNR No 202)** *Louth* **arrives at Victoria Bridge with a train from Derry on 14th August 1959. There is a staff from this cabin, perhaps the very one the signalman is about to offer to the fireman, across the room from me, as I write these words.** John Langford.

Above: **North of Newtownstewart the River Strule changed its name to the Mourne. S class No 62 (GNR No 172)** *Slieve Donard* **is crossing the Mourne near Sion Mills on 8th August 1964 with a train from Belfast to Derry.** Des Fitzgerald.

Right: **The village of Sion Mills was built by the Herdman family who owned the large flax mill which was the village's main source of employment. The mill was close to the station and there was a wagon turntable in the goods yard which enabled railway goods wagons to be brought to the mill for loading and unloading.**
Desmond Coakham.

STRABANE

Top left: **Strabane, like Omagh, was in its day a great railway centre, not that you would know it today, as virtually every trace of the railway has been obliterated by the obligatory by-pass. The Great Northern line entered Strabane on a bridge over the River Mourne. In August 1957 an Apprentice Boys special from Derry hauled by S class No 191** *Croagh Patrick* **leaves the town. Out of sight, to the left of the photographer, is another bridge bringing the County Donegal Railways narrow gauge line to Stranorlar and beyond across the river.** Des Fitzgerald.

Centre left: **The surviving S class locomotive No 171** *Slieve Gullion* **is seen leaving Strabane station in the 1950s with a train bound for Belfast, which is conveying a dining car.** SLS collection.

Below: **At Strabane the CDR narrow gauge system made a junction with the GNR. This view, dating from 5th May 1938, shows the layout at the south end of the station. On the GNR side Q class No 120 is on the 12.40pm from Derry. Both sides of the island platform were used by GNR trains. At the CDR platform, one of that system's early railcars, No 9, forms a service to Stranorlar. The GNR jointly owned the CDR system. The acquisition was made in 1906, in partnership with the English Midland Railway. At the grouping of Britain's railways in 1923, the MR's holding passed to the London, Midland & Scottish Railway.** SLS collection.

Above: **A feature of Strabane was the large board on the up platform listing some of the destinations in County Donegal which could be reached by changing trains here and taking to the narrow gauge lines. These included some places like Burtonport on the Londonderry & Lough Swilly** Railway as well as those on the CDR. S class No 190 *Lugnaquilla* passes the board which is now at the Ulster Folk & Transport Museum. Neil Sprinks.

Below: **Built in 1911, No 165 was the only locomotive of the NLQG class. She is** shunting at the north end of Strabane station. The shed in the distance served both gauges and allowed for the transfer of goods between the two systems. CDR diesel loco *Phoenix* and Railcar No 10, both former Clogher Valley Railway vehicles, can also be seen. John Langford.

JOURNEY'S END

Above: **Leaving Strabane, the line passed into County Donegal and ran close to the west bank of the River Foyle for the remaining 15 miles to Derry. There were** three stations in County Donegal, at Porthall, St Johnston and Carrigans, before the GNR station at Foyle Road was reached. This was the first of the city's four stations, replacing a temporary terminus of 1847, in 1850. Leaving Derry on 25th April 1955 is Q class 4-4-0 No 131 with a train for Belfast.

Below: **Up to the 1960s, some local trains between Strabane and Derry consisted of just a locomotive and a single coach. Such was the formation of the 11.25am from Strabane on 26th June 1952 headed by PPs 4-4-0 No 43, seen passing the goods depot, the site of the L&E station from 1847 to 1850. Both, Neil Sprinks.**

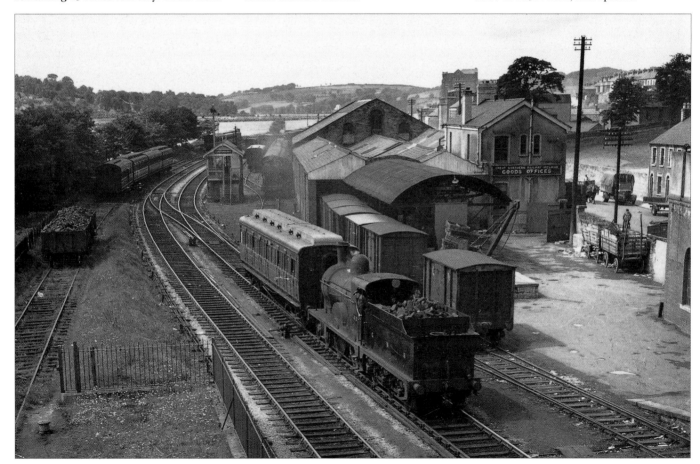

Right: **Another Q class, this time No 130, a type of locomotive long associated with the Derry Road, approaches the station in June 1956.** Neil Sprinks.

Below left: **The exterior of Foyle Road station could best be described as Italianate. Apart from Amiens Street, which offered Italian pastiche on a grand scale, there was nothing quite like this elsewhere on the GNR. On a murky winter day, the frontage looms out of the mist drifting in from the adjacent river.**

Below right: **The station was on a cramped site, hemmed in by the river. On the opposite bank of the River Foyle, steam from a locomotive at the NCC station, Londonderry Waterside, can just be seen below the church in the centre of the picture.** Both, Ian Allan Library.

Bottom right: **Derry had at one time four stations, two broad gauge and two narrow gauge. To shunt the mixed gauge quayside**

lines connecting the GNR at Foyle Road and the Londonderry & Lough Swilly system on the same bank of the Foyle, the Londonderry Port & Harbour Commissioners operated several locomotives over the years. These had two sets of buffers and coupling gear which enabled them to haul wagons on both the 3ft and 5ft 3in gauges. Seen here on the dock lines outside Foyle Road station is LP&HC 0-6-0 saddle tank No 3 *R H Smyth*, **built by the Avonside Engine Company in 1928. This locomotive has been preserved and is in the care of the Railway Preservation Society of Ireland. In the 1990s, when the former NCC main line from Bleach Green to Antrim was being rebuilt, this locomotive was hired by the contractors and used to haul wagons of ballast in connection with the work!** Ian Allan Library.

FROM PORTADOWN TO CAVAN

Top: **Once again our starting point is Portadown Junction. The UR route to Armagh, opened in 1848, forges straight ahead. The line to Derry diverges to the left of the signal box, the Dublin line to the right, passing behind Portadown shed which was in the space between the former UR and D&DJR routes. T2 class 4-4-2 tank No 139 leaves Portadown with a local service to Armagh on 26th May 1956.** Drew Donaldson, courtesy W T Scott.

Above: **Just outside Armagh station, the line to Goraghwood branched off. This section, which lost its passenger trains in 1933, climbed at 1 in 75 from its junction up to Hamiltonsbawn. It was here on 12th June 1889, that an excursion train bound for Warrenpoint stalled on the grade. An attempt to divide the train to take the first section to the summit rendered the brakes ineffective and resulted in the rear ten coaches running away down the grade to crash into the following service train. The death toll of 80 included 22 children. Almost immediately legislation followed, forcing railway companies to make major improvements in operating practices including the introduction of automatic brakes.** Ian Allan Library.

There is a tendency to lump all the lines which were lost in 1957 together because they were closed at the same time and because they connected with each other. To my mind, however, the line from Portadown to Cavan stands apart from the rest of the victims of the 1957 massacre for historical reasons which have always interested me.

The genesis of this route lay in the original 1835 prospectus of the Ulster Railway. For those early railway promoters, a line to the south west of the historical nine county province of Ulster was always their priority. A line to Dublin could be dealt with later. These were practical men embarking on a major enterprise which would involve the raising and spending of great sums of money. It is worth bearing in mind that the UR prospectus was published only five years after the opening of the Liverpool & Manchester Railway, which is generally recognised as the world's first main line railway.

Travellers in pre-famine Ireland often made a favourable contrast between what they found in Ulster and the rest of the country. Ulster was different, it was more prosperous, its peasants often had a more secure type of land tenure and there was some industry. By the 1830s these factors had produced conditions, in the east of the province at least, which were setting it apart from the rest of Ireland. This economic activity was focused on the city of Belfast which was drawing the wealth of its extending hinterland into its warehouses and onto its ships. The famine disrupted much of this progress. Later, political divisions and ultimately the partition of Ireland continued the process.

Despite all of this, in 1952 there were still four through daily weekday trains from Belfast to Cavan, a similar service to that which pertained at the end of the nineteenth century. Compare this with the Irish North line from Dundalk to Derry. In the same timetable there was only one through train from Dundalk to Derry though there were two in the other direction and additional services operated along parts of the route. As well as the passenger trains, there was still a healthy goods traffic along the line. For many in these northern counties which had been in 'the south' since 1923, Belfast was still their city and despite the vicissitudes of history and politics, the customs men and the numerous border crossings, the railway which the vision of those Belfast merchants of the 1830s eventually created was still in place in the 1950s.

ARMAGH

Right: **The attractive exterior of Armagh station, which dated from the opening of the line in 1848, was recorded on 24th August 1957. The UTA buses seen in front of the station will soon have a monopoly of Armagh's public transport with the railway due to close at the end of the following month.** A E Bennett.

Above: **On 11th May 1952, SG2 class 0-6-0 No 15 shunts at the goods yard which was adjacent to the passenger station. Armagh's Roman Catholic cathedral, one of two in the city, which is the ecclesiastical capital of Ireland, dominates the skyline.** SLS collection.

Right: **Entry to Platform No 1 was through the main buildings. This was really the down platform but for the sake of convenience it was often used by trains in both directions. There was also a bay platform on this side of the station, behind the photographer, which had previously been used by trains for the Goraghwood line. In September 1957, PPs class 4-4-0 No 75 is at the head of a local train for Portadown.**
Des Fitzgerald collection.

THE KEADY GOODS

Top left: **In the Introduction reference was made to the shortest-lived stretch of the GNR system, the line from Castleblayney to Armagh, the last built and the first to close. As a through route it lasted only from 1910 to 1923 when the Keady to Castleblayney section was closed completely. Passenger services from Keady to Armagh continued until the end of 1931, but this section remained open for goods traffic until the mass closures of 1957. Here a goods train bound for Keady passes Irish Street Halt on the outskirts of the city, hauled by UG class 0-6-0 No 78.**

Centre left: **This line, which was built largely for reasons of railway politics, to stop possible Midland Great Western incursions into Great Northern territory, involved steep gradients and some heavy engineering. The summit of the line, at Carnagh south of Keady, at 613 feet above sea level, was the highest point on the GNR. There were two viaducts on the line, made from concrete, which of course was a material just coming into its own in the early decades of the twentieth century. The larger of the pair was the 570 foot long, eleven arch Tassagh viaduct, 5½ miles from Armagh. Another UG, No 82 this time, is seen on this viaduct with a short goods train returning to Armagh from Keady.** Both, Drew Donaldson, courtesy W T Scott.

Below left: **Nature was already taking over in the goods yard at Keady on 23rd August 1957, in anticipation of the line's imminent closure, as UG No 80 shunts the wagons it has brought from Armagh.** A E Bennett.

Below: **Though the line was funded by the Great Northern, it was built under the aegis of the Castleblayney, Keady & Armagh Railway Company. This battered enamel warning notice lasted a lot longer than the company and most of the line it built.** Des Fitzgerald.

Above: **Following our brief diversion up the Keady line, we will resume our journey towards Cavan. A short goods train leaves Armagh in the direction of Clones, hauled by UG class 0-6-0 No 82. The station and Armagh station gates can be seen in the background; the line to Keady diverges to the bottom right of the picture.** Drew Donaldson, courtesy W T Scott.

Right: **The first station beyond Armagh was Killylea, about five miles from the city. This view, looking towards Clones, dates from 11th May 1956.** SLS collection.

Bottom right: **Tynan was a distance of some 2½ miles from Killylea. The morning train from Great Victoria Street to Cavan calls there on 3rd July 1957. The leading railcar is No 612. As the GNR usually ran these vehicles in numerically sequential pairs, it is reasonable to assume that the third vehicle in the train, beyond the unpowered trailer in the middle, is No 613! Tynan was the last station in Northern Ireland on this line and it was here that HM Customs officials made their examination of trains.** SLS collection.

Top left: **The line crossed the border and passed from County Armagh into County Monaghan between Tynan and Glaslough. Then, some 27½ miles from Portadown Junction, Monaghan was reached. This county town was served by an impressive station. This view, looking towards Armagh, was taken on 11th May 1956. Customs examinations by Irish officials were conducted here.**

Centre left: **The final station before the important railway crossroads of Clones was reached, was at Smithboro. A three coach railcar set headed by No 605 arrives at the station in this undated view.** Both, SLS collection.

Below: **At Clones East Junction, just outside the station, the former UR line met the Irish North route from Dundalk. On 29th May 1953, an unusual locomotive was recorded hauling the 3.00pm Belfast to Cavan train, seen here arriving at Clones. This was the former LMS/NCC U2 class 4-4-0 No 81 *Carrickfergus Castle*. The GNR hired this locomotive and WT class 2-6-4T No 57 from the UTA in 1952. (No 57 is seen on shed at Adelaide beside No 83 on page 20). No one with whom I have discussed this matter seems to have a definitive answer as to why the locomotives were hired at all, as there is no evidence that the GNR was drastically short of engines at this time. The sight of No 81 at Clones though was quite a coup for the photographer, Neil Sprinks.**

CLONES

Top right: **This view of the exterior of Clones station, dating from 24th August 1957, shows what a large and impressive building it was as befitted an important junction with lines radiating in four directions.** A E Bennett.

Centre right: **At the east end of the station, a three coach railcar set consisting of Nos 617, 616 and a trailer arrive from the Portadown direction on 25th April 1956.** John Edgington.

Below: **The large engine shed at Clones, like that at Portadown, was a half roundhouse made from concrete, built in the 1920s. Access to the shed roads was by a central turntable. The shed was located conveniently for enthusiasts and photographers beside the station. In this busy scene at the west end of the station, recorded on 13th June 1949, the shed is to the left of the picture. The locomotive in the centre of the picture is AL class 0-6-0 No 58 which was the station pilot engine that day. All the platforms are occupied with trains to Belfast, Dublin and Cavan. The latter, to the right of the picture, is headed by QL class 4-4-0 No 157.** SLS collection.

Left: **An AEC railcar set, composed of cars Nos 612, 613 and an intermediate brake has just arrived at Clones having formed the 7.45am service from Belfast in August 1957. Following the complete closure of the part of the Portadown to Cavan line which was in Northern Ireland on the last day of September 1957, CIE maintained a goods and parcels service from Dundalk to Clones, Cavan and Monaghan until December 1959 when this once major rail centre was finally wiped off the railway map of Ireland.** Ian Allan Library.

Below: **A closer view of Clones shed, taken on 27th June 1952. JT class 2-4-2T No 93, built in 1893 and now preserved at the Ulster Folk & Transport Museum, is peeping out of the shed. Some of these**

tank locomotives were based at Clones for use on the Belturbet branch. Railbus No 4, built by the GNR in 1935 for service on the DN&G line, is being turned. The number of each shed road is painted on the wall of the turntable pit.

Left: **West of Clones, the lines to Cavan and Enniskillen ran parallel to each other for about a mile. The Enniskillen line is to the right of No 81 *Carrickfergus Castle*, seen again at Clones, this time on 27th June 1952, arriving with the 11.55am train from Cavan. At this distance in time it is difficult to establish conclusively why No 81 was being used by the GNR. One suggestion is that the company was short of working 4-4-0s at the time. Cavan was certainly a long way off this engine's normal territory.** Both, Neil Sprinks.

BALLYHAISE

Above: **From Clones the Cavan line served Redhills and then reached Ballyhaise, 9 miles from Clones, the junction for the Belturbet branch. On 27th June 1956, QLG class 0-6-0 No 163 approaches the station with a down freight from Clones.** Ian Allan Library.

Top right: **Ballyhaise was a substantial station with three platforms. This view, looking towards Cavan on 13th June 1949, shows QL class 4-4-0 No 24 at the head of the 4.50pm Cavan to Belfast train. A service off the Belturbet branch connected with this train which stopped at all stations to Armagh and did not reach Belfast until after 9.00pm that evening.**

Bottom right: **Trains on the Belturbet branch were often mixed, conveying both passenger coaches and goods wagons. Typical of such workings is this view of a service ready to leave Ballyhaise for Belturbet on 13th June 1949. JT class 2-4-2T No 92 is at the head of a formation which consists of a bogie and a six wheel coach and a few goods wagons, with a goods brake van bringing up the rear.** Both, SLS collection.

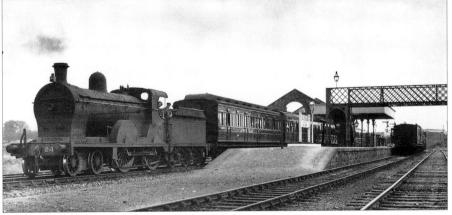

BELTURBET

Above: **There were no intermediate stations on the 4½ mile long branch from Ballyhaise to Belturbet. At the terminus there was cross platform interchange between the GNR and the 3ft gauge Cavan & Leitrim section of CIE. On 13th May 1952, JT class No 94 is the engine working the GNR branch. At the other platform is the former Tralee & Dingle Railway 2-6-2T No 5, built by Hunslet in 1892. This locomotive, which has been preserved, was transferred by CIE to the C&L in 1950. The narrow gauge connection was not advertised in the GNR timetables of the 1940s and 50s. Perhaps this was just as well, as by this time there was only one narrow gauge working conveying passengers in each direction on the northern part of the C&L which served Belturbet.**

Centre left: **In this view dating from August 1937, we see the transshipment siding and shed at Belturbet. The narrow gauge engine shed is to the right of the picture. The train shed of the GNR station is on the far left of the picture, to its right is the GNR goods shed.** Both, SLS collection.

Bottom left: **The concept of an integrated transport system has been widely advocated in recent years. A GNR lorry is seen making deliveries in Belturbet in the late 1950s, proving there is nothing new under the sun.** John Langford.

CAVAN

Top right: **What was to become the GNR line to Cavan was opened in 1862. The town already had a rail service dating back to 1856 when the MGWR line from Inny Junction, on that company's Mullingar to Sligo route, was opened. The two companies shared the same station and there was a connection between them. On 13th June 1949, QL class No 24 prepares to leave Cavan with the 4.50pm train to Clones and Belfast.**

Centre right: **The station layout at Cavan was strange. The main platform had only a single track. The other platform made it effectively a bay. About half way down its length, beside the signal box, the track was bridged by a footway at platform level which marked the boundary between the GNR and CIE territory. GNR U class 4-4-0 No 197 *Lough Neagh*, built by Beyer Peacock in 1915 but not named until 1949, is seen at the GNR end of the platform with a local service to Clones.**

Below: **On 11th May 1956, Railbus No 1, another GNR survivor which can be seen at the Ulster Folk & Transport Museum, arrives at Cavan with the 12.25pm service from Clones. The GNR goods shed is seen in the distance.** All photos on this page, SLS collection.

THE IRISH NORTH

The final part of our Great Northern journey takes us along the tracks of the former Irish North Western Railway. Though the INWR lost its independent identity when it amalgamated with the other companies to form the GNR in the 1870s, its name lived on in the vocabulary of railway workers and railway enthusiasts who continued to refer to this part of the GNR as the Irish North.

This was the long cross country route from Dundalk, on the east coast, to Bundoran, on the west. By the time of the formation of the GNR,

all of these lines were being worked by the INWR. Though there were through workings from Dundalk to Derry and of course the Irish North was traversed by the famous 'Bundoran Express', which ran from Dublin to the County Donegal resort, most passenger services covered part of the route rather than all of it. Many services began or terminated at Enniskillen which had trains to Dundalk and Omagh or on to Derry, and to Bundoran. Most trains stopped at all stations and timings were not exacting. The 'Bundoran Express' in the summer timetable of

1952 took 70 minutes for the 40 miles from Dundalk to Clones; an all-stations train on the same section could take as long as 98 minutes.

Whilst not strictly speaking part of the GNR, though the company did work the route from 1933, we will begin this chapter with a glance at the Dundalk, Newry & Greenore line which made an end-on junction with the GNR at Dundalk and whose trains later used the GNR station there. This line is too interesting a footnote to the GNR to ignore.

THE DUNDALK, NEWRY & GREENORE RAILWAY

Above: **The first part of the DN&G, from Dundalk to Greenore, was opened in 1873. It was followed in 1876 by a line from Greenore to Newry. The lines were funded by the English London & North Western Railway which was keen to develop the port of Greenore to increase its already large share of the cross channel trade. It was as if a part of the LNWR was shipped across the Irish Sea and then unpacked. Signs and signals, locomotives and rolling stock all bore the stamp of Euston and Crewe. The DN&G passed to the LMS in 1923, who found**

themselves with a line which was now, since the partition of Ireland, in a foreign country. The GNR took over the working of the lines in 1933 but its LNWR character persisted. On 20th May 1949, the morning train from Greenore is seen passing LNWR signals near Dundalk Barrack Street. It consists of four LNWR six wheelers in LNWR livery, which had not been used in England since 1923. The engine is 0-6-0 saddletank No 3 *Dundalk*, built at Crewe in 1873. John Dewing.

Right and opposite page: **The DN&G boundary marker at Dundalk Barrack Street was still in place in August 1958. The other side of the marker, still bearing the initials INWRy, is seen on the page opposite.** Both, A E Bennett.

Top right: **In the years after 1933 when the Great Northern took over both the working and the maintenance of the DN&G lines, GNR locomotives, often the JT class 2-4-2Ts, were to be seen working DN&G services. The now preserved No 93, built at Dundalk in 1893, is seen leaving Bellurgan station with a Greenore to Dundalk train on 28th December 1951, just a few days before the line closed.** Ian Allan Library.

Centre right: **The INWR/GNR goods depot at Dundalk Barrack Street remained in use until the mid 1990s. SG3 class 0-6-0 No 40 was shunting here on 20th June 1958. The DN&G running line is just out of view to the left of the picture beyond the goods shed.** A E Bennett.

Bottom: **The physical junction between the two lines was at Windmill Lane between Barrack Street and the DN&G station at Dundalk Quay Street. DN&G trains ran through to the GNR station and this involved them passing over the GNR main line on the level at Dundalk Square Crossing. On 15th May 1950 JT class 2-4-2T No 90 is seen on the crossing with a train from Greenore to Dundalk.** H C Casserley.

Above: **In February 1948, a train bound for Enniskillen leaves Dundalk station at the start of its 62 mile long journey. At Dundalk Central cabin it will branch off the main line to the right to take the Irish North route. The locomotive at the head of the train, the brand new U class 4-4-0 No 203 *Armagh*, had only been delivered by Beyer Peacock the previous month. When built, these engines had screw couplings on the front buffer. This was later replaced by a three link coupling. The abbreviation Nº was also soon removed from their front buffer beams, leaving just the number.** Ian Allan Library.

Centre left: **Inniskeen was 7 miles from Dundalk. In 1886 it became the junction for the 6½ mile long branch to Carrickmacross. In this undated view, an 0-6-0 is shunting the branch goods at the station. The branch lost its passenger services in March 1947, but goods traffic continued until the end of 1959, when CIE closed the remaining parts of the Irish North and the Clones to Monaghan line.** SLS collection.

Bottom left: **There was just one intermediate station on the line at Essexford, which was roughly half way along the branch. PG class 0-6-0 No 102, built in 1901, pauses at the station with a cattle train. The station name was picked out in white stones on the bank opposite the platform. This locally inspired decoration was a feature of several other GNR country stations.** Drew Donaldson, courtesy W T Scott.

CARRICKMACROSS

Right: **Carrickmacross station had all the facilities that one would expect at the terminus of a country branch line. The signal cabin and the goods yard to the left of the picture are seen in this August 1957 view. The by then disused passenger station is also visible in the distance. This part of the world developed something of a reputation for smuggling after the Irish border was established. An old rhyme went, 'from Carrickmacross to Crossmaglen, there are more rogues than honest men.' I am sure this reputation was unwarranted, but that does not stop me from repeating it!** A E Bennett.

Above: **QG class 0-6-0 No 153 is running round the coaches of the branch train on 27th June 1939. The station is similar in layout to other GNR branch termini we have seen, such as those at Ardee, Oldcastle and Warrenpoint. The train shed offers excellent protection to passengers and the station is built in the yellow brick which was used to construct so many GNR stations.** SLS collection.

Right: **Back on the main line, the first stopping place north west of Inniskeen was Blackstaff Halt. The attractive station at Culloville, seen here, was the next location, 12 miles from Dundalk.** SLS collection.

CASTLEBLAYNEY

Above: **Castleblayney was the first sizeable town served by the line, after it left** **Dundalk. A short section of the erstwhile CK&A line, which closed in 1923 (see page 84) survived as a siding up to the closure of the line to Clones in 1959. It is seen here diverging to the right at Castleblayney West cabin.** John Langford.

Below: **By the date this picture was taken, 31st July 1958, only goods and parcels traffic remained. Boxes of fish are being unloaded from railcar C₁'s trailer at Castleblayney, but the town no longer has a passenger service.** Ian Allan Library.

Right: **Ballybay was 7 miles west of Castleblayney. Like a number of stations on the Irish North, this had just one platform on the main line. The bay to the right of the picture was used by trains off the 7½ mile long Cootehill branch. This left the Clones line at Shantonagh Junction, 2 miles west of Ballybay. The branch opened in 1860, lost its passenger service in 1947 and closed completely in 1955.**

Below: **Given its remoteness and the fact that it closed at a relatively early date to passengers, photos of the Cootehill branch are not common. This view of the terminus, with QG class 0-6-0 No 154 at the head of the branch train which consisted of only a couple of six wheelers, probably dates from the late 1930s.** Both, SLS collection.

Right: **As we dealt with Clones in some detail in the previous chapter, we will literally skirt round it here as U class No 199 *Lough Derg* leaves the town on 27th June 1952 with one of the few through workings from Derry to Dundalk. You would not have wanted to be in a hurry if you used this service. It left Derry at 6.55am calling at all stations to Omagh. Leaving there at 8.25am, its leisurely progress continued as it called at all stations to Enniskillen and Dundalk. If running to time, it would have left Clones at 10.55am. A passenger who joined the train at Derry would now have been on board for four hours, with another 100 minutes to enjoy before Dundalk was reached at 12.35pm!** Neil Sprinks.

Left: **After leaving Clones, the line crossed the border from County Monaghan into County Fermanagh. The first station in Northern Ireland was Newtownbutler where H M Customs examined trains. With both the United Kingdom and the Irish Republic now members of the European Union, the Irish border, whilst it still has a strong political reality, is no longer the economic impediment it once was. The memory of the delays to cross border travel and commerce, so long imposed by customs examinations is fading.** SLS collection.

Below: **Like so many Irish lines, the Irish North was peppered with level crossings. In the nineteenth century the modest cost**

of a gate keeper's wages was a more attractive proposition than the capital cost of building a bridge. The custodians of Sallaghy crossing, one of eight on the 7¼ mile stretch between Newtownbutler and Lisnaskea, will not be troubled by the care of their gates much longer, as a lifting train hauled on 19th May 1960 by SG No 183 performs its melancholy duty. Drew Donaldson, courtesy W T Scott.

Bottom left: **Lisnaskea station, looking here in the direction of Enniskillen, was recorded on 11th May 1956. The similarities between its main building and that at Newtownbutler are apparent. These D&E stations are quite different from those seen elsewhere on the GNR.** SLS collection.

Above: **Four level crossings and 2½ miles on from Lisnaskea, was Maguiresbridge. Until its closure in 1941, this was the junction for the Clogher Valley narrow gauge line which meandered for 37 miles through Fermanagh and Tyrone to the GNR station at Tynan. SG3 No 14 hauls a** long cattle train from Enniskillen to Belfast through the station on 3rd July 1957. Cattle traffic, much of it originating from the Sligo, Leitrim & Northern Counties line at Enniskillen, was an important source of revenue on this route. SLS collection.

Below: **Lisbellaw was the final station before Enniskillen 5 miles distant. Again here, one platform sufficed. Unusually here the up starter and and down home signals were both positioned on the same post.** Ian Allan Library.

ENNISKILLEN

Left: **S class No 174 *Carrantuohill* heads south from Enniskillen on Sunday 29th June 1956 with a Gaelic Athletic Association special taking supporters to a big match at Clones. It was unusual to see S class locomotives at work on the Irish North, these handsome machines spent most of their time on the main line and the Derry Road. Whilst they had little else in common, both the GAA and the Loyal Orders were great supporters of the railways. Special trains in conjunction with football and hurling matches, and to bring the brethren to demonstrations, were often run.** Neil Sprinks.

Above: **Enniskillen shed was located at the south end of the station opposite the divergence of the SLNCR line. It was usually host to a number of the lighter 4-4-0s such as the U and P classes and a few 0-6-0s. On 31st May 1954, QL class 4-4-0 No 126 arrives at Enniskillen on the 10.45am train from Dundalk. On shed is blue liveried U class No 202 *Louth*.** Neil Sprinks.

Left: **The imposing exterior of Enniskillen station is seen in this view taken the month before closure, on 15th August 1957.** A E Bennett.

Right: **It is appropriate here to have a brief encounter with the GNR's neighbour at Enniskillen, the SLNCR. (May I refer those wishing to know more about this delightful line to Neil Sprinks' excellent book in this series.) SLNCR passenger trains used the bay platforms at the south end of the station. In the post-war years almost all passenger services were in the hands of railbuses and the line's 1947-built Walker railcar. The railbuses usually hauled a light trailer for parcels and luggage. Here railbus 2A, acquired from the GNR in 1938, and its trailer, sit in the bay at Enniskillen.** Ian Allan Library.

Below: **This view shows the SLNCR yard at Enniskillen. The running line is that to the right of the brake coach in the centre of**

the picture. In this June 1937 view, the two sheds are occupied by steam locomotives. In later years the railcar usually lived in one of these when it was not out on the line. SLS collection.

Right: **Among the line's many quirks was the fact that the locomotives were known by name only, they never carried numbers. The now preserved 0-6-4 tank *Lough Erne*, built by Beyer Peacock in 1949, is shunting vans, including the inevitable cattle wagon, at Enniskillen in May 1954. Cattle traffic was a mainstay of the SLNCR's business. This was handed over to the GNR at Enniskillen for onward transit to the east coast ports and ultimately the dinner tables of England.** Ian Allan Library.

Top: **For those interested in railways, the highlight of the day at Enniskillen was probably the passage of the Irish North's very own named train, the 'Bundoran Express'. The term 'express' should not be taken too literally in relation to this train. In the summer of 1952, the down train** left Dublin at 8.45am but did not reach Bundoran until 2.00pm, taking 5¼ hours for the distance of about 160 miles. It ran non-stop through Northern Ireland, from Clones to Pettigo. This meant that it had to grind slowly round the severe curve through Enniskillen station. Here 1915 built U class No 199 *Lough Derg* is in charge of this up working.

Above: **Back at the main platform, we see the 6.40pm passenger train about to head north to Omagh hauled by PPs 4-4-0 No 74.** Both, SLS collection.

Right: **Enniskillen station, built on a five chain curve, was opened by the D&E in 1860, replacing the earlier L&E one of 1854, which was further to the north. On 4th July 1955, Q class No 136, in the platform to the right, has arrived with the 10.50am from Omagh. The train at the other platform is the 12 noon service to Omagh.** SLS collection.

Above: **On 31st May 1954, a train for Pettigo leaves Enniskillen hauled by PPs class 4-4-0 No 74. The pillar on the high ground in the distance is Cole's Monument. This was erected in honour of a distinguished general, Sir Galbraith Lowry Cole, who hailed from County Fermanagh and served with Wellington in the Peninsular War. Those brave enough to climb the 108 steps of the spiral staircase inside the pillar were rewarded with fine panoramic views over the town, Lough Erne and of course the railway station.** Neil Sprinks.

Right: **Another PPs class locomotive, No 106, has a good head of steam as it leaves Enniskillen with a service for Omagh on 31st May 1954.** Neil Sprinks.

Above: **On the outskirts of Enniskillen, on 2nd June 1954, PPs class 4-4-0 No 106 heads the 4.18pm train from Omagh made up of four coaches and a collection of vans, with two cattle wagons bringing up the rear.**

Below: **In June 1956 the down 'Bundoran Express' is passing Ballinamallard. An elderly black liveried Ps class 4-4-0 No 73, built in 1895, is in charge, perhaps replacing a failed U class engine which was the normal motive power for this** train which served both holidaymakers heading for the fleshpots of Bundoran and penitents bound for the rigours of St Patrick's Purgatory on an island in the middle of Lough Derg near Pettigo station. Both, Neil Sprinks.

BUNDORAN JUNCTION

Right: **Bundoran Junction, 8 miles from Enniskillen and 35 miles from Bundoran, was located close to the hamlet of Kilskeery. It was a triangular junction, though there were only platforms on two sides of the triangle. In this view taken on 14th June 1949, the line from Enniskillen to Bundoran is on the left, the route to Omagh on the right. The third side of the triangle allowed through running from Omagh in the direction of Bundoran, avoiding the station. Scheduled passenger services did not use this curve which was largely the preserve of goods and excursion trains. Here the 10.15am from Bundoran, hauled by small wheeled**

Ps class 4-4-0 No 105, has arrived at the junction. This was another tight curve for the 'Bundoran Express' to negotiate. Still running non-stop, it had to travel a further 15 miles to Pettigo before it could draw breath. SLS collection.

Above: **On 2nd June 1954, PPs class No 42 with the 10.30am from Bundoran takes the line towards the station at Bundoran Junction West cabin. The tracks to the right formed the third side of the triangle, by-passing the station and allowing through running from the Bundoran line towards Omagh.** Neil Sprinks.

Right: **The down 'Bundoran Express' accelerates away from the junction headed by one of the later batch of U class 4-4-0s, No 203 *Armagh*.** John Edgington collection.

THE BUNDORAN LINE

Top left: **The Bundoran line opened in 1866. The first station on the branch was at Irvinestown; indeed for a few years before the line opened, Bundoran Junction was called Irvinestown Road though the town was about 3 miles away. Just under 10 miles from the Junction was Kesh. PPs class 4-4-0 No 50 arrives at this station on an up train.** Ian Allan Library.

Centre left: **Passengers crowd the platform at Pettigo on 27th July 1957 as the up 'Bundoran Express' arrives at the station hauled by U class No 203 *Armagh*. The village of Pettigo straddles the border. Most of it is in County Fermanagh in Northern Ireland but its station was in County Donegal, in the Irish Republic. Running this train in both directions non-stop between here and Clones avoided the need for customs examinations. The up and down trains crossed at Pettigo. Whilst the 'Bundoran Express' was used by holidaymakers heading for the popular resort of Bundoran, where the Great Northern had an hotel, most of these passengers waiting for the train at Pettigo had other priorities. They will have spent several days fasting and praying on an island on Lough Derg, not far from Pettigo. The lough, which has associations with Saint Patrick, was a place of pilgrimage for devout Catholics. The regime on the island was severe, black tea and dry bread being the main sustenance offered to penitents during their stay. Someone who made the pilgrimage to the island once told me that the hardest privation to bear was the smell of frying bacon coming from the kitchen of the priests' house in the morning. When the Bundoran line closed, the nearest railhead to Lough Derg was Omagh. CIE used to run a special train from Dublin for the pilgrims who completed their journey by bus, a latter day pale shadow of the 'Bundoran Express'. This working brought CIE 141 class General Motors diesels to the Derry Road in its final years.**

Bottom left: **The line crossed back into Northern Ireland shortly after leaving Pettigo and ran close to the shores of Lough Erne serving Castlecaldwell and then Belleek, the final station in County Fermanagh, where PPs class 4-4-0 No 50 is seen on a passenger train. Belleek is famous for the fine pottery which is made there and no doubt many a consignment was carefully dispatched from the station in GNR vans.** Both, Drew Donaldson, courtesy W T Scott.

Right: **After leaving Belleek, the line crossed the River Erne, back into County Donegal. The penultimate station on the line was Ballyshannon. This town was served by two railways on two different gauges. A branch of the County Donegal narrow gauge system, from Donegal Town, reached Ballyshannon in 1905. The CDR terminus was on the other side of the town, over a mile from the GNR station. On a sunny 1st June 1954, the 10.30am Bundoran to Enniskillen train leaves Ballyshannon hauled by PPs class 4-4-0 No 74. The bright yellow gorse, common in many parts of Ireland during the summer, lights up the cutting.** Neil Sprinks.

Below: **On 3rd July 1957, PPs class No 44 pauses at Ballyshannon station with the 2.35pm service from Bundoran Junction to Bundoran.** SLS collection.

Right: **Bundoran was one of many small seaside towns dotted along the coasts of these islands which owed its prosperity to the coming of the railway. It was never meant to be a terminus; the intention was to extend the line the 20 odd miles to Sligo, completing a line down the west coast as far as Limerick. Sadly this never happened. Here the 2.35pm from the Junction is seen arriving at Bundoran on 8th May 1956. PPs No 43, built at Dundalk in 1911, has acquired one of the modern tenders supplied to run with the UG class engines built in 1948. Her coaches are also of interest. These are two of the ex-London & North Western Railway vehicles bought by the GNR in 1948.** SLS collection.

Above: **We are back at Bundoran Junction for the final leg of our trip around the Great Northern system. A train for Omagh leaves the junction hauled by U class 4-4-0 No 205** *Down*. **The tracks to the right of the picture are those which allowed trains from the Omagh direction to run through to the Bundoran line without calling at the station. The formation behind the locomotive is very typical of those which slowly trundled along the Irish North calling at most stations en route. A six wheel van is followed by two carriages, one of them a brake. Next is one of the GNR's bogie P vans, and the tail of the train is made up of a collection of vans and bread containers.** John Edgington collection.

Above left: **Trillick, 1½ miles from Bundoran Junction, was the first station on the line towards Omagh. On 12th May 1953, PPs class 4-4-0 No 74 is seen at the station whose facilities were fairly basic. It was well looked after, and the name, picked out on the grassy bank, is an attractive feature of the station.** SLS collection.

Bottom left: **Experienced railway travellers in Ireland would have known to be wary of stations which had the word 'Road' in their name. It usually implied that the station was a considerable distance from the place it was supposed to serve. This was certainly the case with Dromore Road, which was about 3 miles from the small County Tyrone village from which it took its name. Ps No 73 is seen at Dromore Road on what is known in Ireland as a soft day, meaning that it is raining!** Ian Allan Library.

Above: **Of the four forms of traction employed by the GNR in the 1950s, we have already seen steam and diesel aplenty, and the electric tramcars on the Hill of Howth will be considered in the final chapter. That leaves the Fintona branch and its famous horse tram to complete the picture. Fintona Junction was about 7 miles from Omagh. As the impecunious L&E was slowly extending its line towards Enniskillen, funds ran out in 1853 as the small village of Fintona in County Tyrone was reached. When work began again the following year, it was decided that a better route could be made from what became Fintona Junction. The company got permission to work the short branch down to the village, which was only about three quarters of a mile in extent, using a horse tram and this arrangement continued until the line closed in 1957. On 3rd July 1957, P class 4-4-0 No 105 is seen on an Enniskillen to Omagh train. The horse tram is waiting to make the connection to the village. The horse is still in the stable on the other side of the signal box.** SLS collection.

Centre right: **The tram leaves the junction hauled by** *Dick*, **the last of a long line of equine motive power used on the branch. The tram itself had accommodation for all three classes. First and Second Class passengers were allowed inside under cover, those in Third Class were banished to the top deck.** Neil Sprinks.

Bottom right: **Steam engines were allowed down the branch to work the goods traffic. The tram is seen here ready to return to the junction from Fintona station.** Ian Allan Library.

TRAMS AND BUSES

Above left: **In these last few pages we will visit the GNR's famous Hill of Howth Tramway and have space to no more than acknowledge the extensive network of bus routes which the company operated.**

Opened in 1901 at a cost of £100,000, the 5ft 3in gauge Hill of Howth Tramway, which was electrified on a 550 volts DC overhead trolley system, connected the stations of Howth and Sutton via a 5¼ mile loop over the Hill of Howth. Reputedly the line lost money throughout its 58 year lifespan. Used more by excursionists than commuters, fortunately, it did not lead to building all over the scenic hill, as the GNR might have hoped. The line was single track with passing loops. Two cars led by No 5 head down to Howth through the loop at Dungriffan Road.

Above right: **On the other side of the summit was the loop at Bailey Post Office where a wooden waiting shelter was provided.** Both, Neil Sprinks.

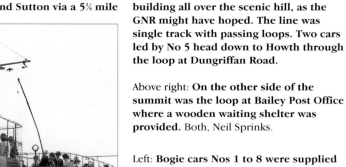

Left: **Bogie cars Nos 1 to 8 were supplied by Brush of Loughborough for the opening of the line. In 1902 a further two cars, Nos 9 and 10, which were larger than the Brush cars, came from Milnes of Birkenhead. The latter were never as popular as the first cars and seem to have been used mostly when the line was very busy. Latterly Nos 1 to 8 were painted in the GNR railcar blue and cream livery. Nos 9 and 10 carried a teak livery, similar to that used on GNR carriages. No 10 and 4 are at the Summit on a busy 18th May 1959, in the last days of the tramway.** John Edgington.

Top left: **On a grey day in March 1954, with no one on the top deck, No 5 rumbles along Strand Road in Sutton on the way to the Summit.** Neil Sprinks.

Top right: **Car No 2 was at Sutton on 24th April 1951. The footbridge of the station is in the background.** John Edgington.

Right: **Both the depot and the power station were at Sutton. No 1 and the line's Works car, No 11, are seen outside the depot.** Ian Allan Library.

Below: **This is the GNR in all its pomp, 1948 style! Butlin's opened a holiday camp at Mosney near Drogheda and the GNR built a station to serve it. In this wonderful posed period piece, the 'Enterprise Express' is on the main line and happy campers are about to embark on a coach tour in this lovely GNR AEC Regal.** Ian Allan Library.

Left: **The GNR operated an extensive network of bus services in the Irish Republic. About 90 routes are listed in the 1952 Summer Railway Timetable. The company had also operated bus services in Northern Ireland until 1935 when legislation setting up the Northern Ireland Road Transport Board prohibited railway companies from running buses in the province. GNR buses were still seen in Northern Ireland on cross border routes originating in the Republic. The routes operated by GNR buses ranged from city services in north Dublin to remote locations like Glenties in County Donegal. Though the branch from Ardee to Dromin Junction lost its passenger services in 1934, the County Louth town continued to be served by GNR buses. An AEC double decker on the Drogheda to Ardee route is seen at Drogheda station on 20th August 1957.** A E Bennett.

Above: **There is time for these GNR busmen to have a yarn as the customs men do their worst at the Killeen Customs Post on the main Dublin to Belfast road. The AEC double decker is on a service from Dundalk to Newry.** Ian Allan Library.

Left: **This bus seen at Enniskillen station in 1957 worked a Cavan to Enniskillen via Belturbet service. GNR buses were painted in the blue and cream livery which was also applied to the railcars and to eight of the ten Hill of Howth trams. Though these few views are no more than an acknowledgement of the GNR's bus services, and for reasons of space, the company's road freight vehicles have scarcely featured in these pages at all, I hope that it will be remembered that the GNR was offering its customers 50 or more years ago, something which is only now being rediscovered: a fully integrated transport service. Enterprising in so many things, the dear old GNR was way ahead of its time.** F W Shuttleworth.